Daughter Drink This Water

Also by Jaiya John

Freedom: Medicine Words for your Brave Revolution
Calm: Inspiration for a Possible Life
Sincerity of Sunlight: A Book of Inspiration
Fresh Peace: Daily Blossoming of the Soul
Your Caring Heart: Renewal for Helping Professionals and Systems
Clear Moon Tribe
The Day Jumoke Found His Name
Legendary: A Tribute to Those Who Honorably Serve Devalued Children
Beautiful: A Poetic Celebration of Displaced Children
Reflection Pond: Nurturing Wholeness in Displaced Children
Habanero Love: A Poem of Sacred Passion
Father to Son: Ode to Black Boys
Lyric of Silence: A Poetic Telling of the Human Soul Journey
Black Baby White Hands: A View from the Crib

DAUGHTER DRINK THIS WATER

JAIYA JOHN

Soul Water Rising

Camarillo, California

Printed in the United States of America

Soul Water Rising
Camarillo, California
http://www.soulwater.org

Library of Congress Control Number: 2021901238
ISBN 978-0-9987802-4-5

First Soul Water Rising Edition, Hardcover: 2021

Inspiration / Affirmation / Self Care

Editors: Jacqueline V. Carter
            Kent W. Mortensen

Cover & Interior Design: Jaiya John

Daughter. I am going to tell you a secret:
You are the best thing that ever happened to you.
When you feel this, and know this, you will be free.

Jaiya John

Arrival

Many believed he was thousands of years old.

A gentle breeze filled the valley that day. Girls and women of all ages moved quietly into the long, broad meadow. They were a delta of energy. The ancient one sat at the head of the meadow, on a hillside, shaded by an acacia tree. The women had sent for him. They needed their prayers spoken back to them and their daughters, through one of the ancient, Loving ones. So they could remember.

The people had come from all over the land, granting themselves this moment. A strong river of knowing ran through their bones. At first, rumors of the ancient one's coming trickled from woman to woman, more as a hope. Soon, the young girls dreamed him. They began to ask their mothers, aunties, and grandmas, *Is it true? Is he coming to be with us?* It was this intuition of girls that caused the women to take the possibility solemnly.

They knew he was beyond man or woman, even as he walked, a man. They whispered about him. *I heard he is a jokester. I heard his tears cause monsoons. I heard he is an arthritic monk. A shape shifter. Stands with trees at night. Eats moonlight.*

And now, here he was. And here they were, pouring into the bright valley, not knowing what to expect, yet pulled by a growing sense of something *in them* that would change everything.

Some heard his voice as thunder on this cloudless day in a land where the sky hangs low. Others experienced a gentle whisper, yet others a tidal strength. He spoke in every language, the old ones and the new. They each heard him in the language closest to their personal hearts. Some heard him in the language of silence.

He spoke:

Daughters. You are here with me. I cannot say my gratitude. Please excuse the timing of my arrival. I am not as young as I used to be, nor as old as I used to be. I am as my body decided for this day.

Let my words be not a heavy sky weighing on you, but rather a bright breeze lifting you, easing your heart. I am not teaching, I am praying. These words are my prayer.

I am not telling you what you do not know. I am lifting it up for you. Your truth lives in you always. In some seasons of your life you see it clearly. Other times life's sediment buries it. Now I lift your personal truth to you, my offering. Because I Love you, I do not wish to shape you. I care to see you free yourself into your own, forever dancing, changing shape.

I pray you know my words are soaked in Love. They *are* Love. Love is truth. I pray to offer you medicine for your healing. For your miracle of a beautiful life.

I have come to share the river of my life with you, and to learn your ways, your medicine and stories. Together, let us hold the sacred fire.

Daughters, I need you to bless me with your truth. That I may return it to you through this soul of mine that has seen many times. Come now. Join with me.

The valley of girls and women poured over him. Those in reach embraced him. The rest embraced him by embracing each other. His body disappeared into them. They began to hum. It was ancient. Sky stopped. The valley of bodies trembled. Far away birds sang their recognition of this gathering. After a long moment, the people began to pull back from him, returning to their spots. They sat in the trees, and on the sweetgrass, and grouped along the river and on the swells of earth.

Now he was no longer a body, but a mound of tears. Theirs and his. The gossamer tears solidified. His body reemerged. It was full of their truth, which he released. His voice swelled with emotion. Looking to the sky, he spoke an offering:

Creator, fill this solemn valley with a sky that aches its memory out into the trees. Let them weep a mist of fine reunion. A gathering of mountains, that particular tribe of creatures who rise and fall over ages, and bury generations of story in their soil. To our four elements, we give this offering. To our four teachers we pay reverence. To the four directions we turn, our knees in the black earth, and pray: *May we breathe the air of this ordained cusp of morning and become water. Worthy of living as the purity of tears.*

He spoke again to the valley of women:

I am not your father saying this truth. I am all the fathers of all your fathers, all the mothers of all your mothers, all the ancestors of all your ancestors. I am your children after you who need you whole. I am Creator, creation, created. Love and its pure language speaking *you* to you.

I am the son of a daughter. I speak as the son and his prior generations of sons. I also speak as the daughter and her prior generations of daughters. Please do not be misled by my appearance. I have long ago left behind the enslaving myths of woman and man, the insecure labeling of spirit too feral to be corralled. If you say I cannot know womanhood, you define my fatherhood as a narrow strip of dead land insulated from the world.

Womanhood lives in my fatherhood. Not in the way it lives in you. In the way it lives in me as a father. I am not infiltrated by womanhood. It is not a trickling of streams into my land. Womanhood is an aspect of my manhood, not a separate water. Think of rivers that enter and even flow through the ocean. You cannot say the ocean is not those rivers, or that those rivers are not the ocean. Only that each cannot know the entire truth of the other.

I speak as your father. My motives are those of a father. If you want another perspective, please seek that source. Be aware that you will be receiving other motives, and who knows what that intent will be? My intent is Love. Not obsession, possession, or oppression. I do not care to guide you. Your path belongs to you and your Creator, a force much more knowing than I. I care to feed you. With a faith that as you are fed you will grow, and you will become what you always were, the pristine truth that sang and danced before this world became.

I do not presume to know womanhood. I presume to know suffering. Self rejection. And the arduous journey to Love and wholeness. I presume to share through my vessel the testimony of endless souls I have known and witnessed. To remove myself from their telling as best as I am able, so my vessel is clean for what comes through. I cannot tell you how to be a woman. I can, with my infinite Love, nurture you into Loving the woman you are.

Your Sacredness

The ancient one spoke with a depth of prayer:

Something immeasurably divine, sacred, and miraculous is happening right now. You are happening. You are alive. Much of life comes down to two questions: What do you consider sacred? How do you treat your sacred things?

You are a sacred land. This means everything. People cannot treat you however they wish. Nor can you treat yourself according to any impulse or mood. You are a place where ancestors rest and ceremonies are performed. You are sacred water, fire, sky, earth.

The first act in a beautiful life is to recognize the truth of who and what you are. You are sacredness. As long as you stay in this truth, you may have your beautiful life. This world will often act to persuade you otherwise. It will whisper and shout that you are not sacred, that you are less than that. Your entire life will be a soulful struggle to remember your sacredness, to stay in it.

You are a salmon swimming upstream against a degrading current that wants your soul. You were born to swim upstream to spawn beauty in your life and feed generations their own chance to live. Always upstream, always against a current. This can be hard. It can be the sweetest journey.

Our great misunderstanding is that we believe some things are meant to be done soullessly, and other things soulfully. Gradually, this line creeps. More and more we live soullessly, believing it to be the easier way. Nothing is meant to be lived soullessly. Ease has nothing to do with it. You are a soulful thing. Live soulfully.

You are woman. This means you must engage in a revolution just to be whole. A revolution inside yourself.

If the revolution tires you, such is the price for freedom. For slavery brings an exhaustion that makes revolution seem like a revival.

Things will try to enter you, to take your earth, own your land. Do not be passive with your glory, nor hard, turned to stone. You can be soft and still protect your sacredness. Sky, for example, or the way you weave your Love.

Because you are a portal, many people, confused as to their own purpose, will confuse you for a thing to be used, owned, exploited. Any living thing targeted for exploitation is in grave danger if it does not know how to protect its sacredness. Anger and hardness may come to mind as weapons. But if you are always preparing for war, you will invite war, and war will be the only thing of which you are capable. Prepare for Love. Garden your softness, kindness, heart strength, and soul force. Prepare to be open. Prepare for your assertion and aura.

This world wants to desecrate you. Stay sacred. Use as your examples those who live sacredly. Don't wallow in unwellness and hope to be well. Stand in the rain if you want to be cleansed. Don't seek shelter the moment you see rainclouds. Go to what cures you. Live with it.

You don't have to be a queen, princess, or any other royalty to value yourself or be treated honorably. Having a title isn't vital. Royalty is an artificial elevation, filled with rampant superiority and inferiority, ego and submission. In your sacredness you are not above or beneath any soul. Your value and worth don't come from adulation, idolizing, or worship. They come from your essential truth. Your existence is priceless regardless of applause or praise. Your price cannot be raised.

Remember yourself. Those who want to control you, to use you, need first and foremost for you to forget who you are, forget your divine assignment, your sacred nature, your ancestral inheritance. Your amnesia is their victory. Without your memory, you are a helpless prey on a broad, merciless prairie. But if you build a fire of memory, and you keep it, you will have fire to keep away the predators. You will have your own light, to see yourself and your wilderness. Remember you. This will be your anchor, your compass, your fortress.

Your vulnerability is a garden. If you take care of your garden, your vulnerability becomes a glorious treasure. And if you neglect your garden, your vulnerability becomes a graveyard. All your promise dies there. What makes you vulnerable? Your holy river of tears. Your tenderness. Your ethic of justice, of caring that other living things not suffer.

Always honor yourself. In doing so, you honor your people, your ancestors, your descendants, and your time on earth. Live with dignity, grace, integrity, and nobility. And Love yourself. This world wants to take things from you as a woman. Most of all it wants to take your self Love. Once it has that, it has you. Stay free. You belong to you. You are a sovereign soul. Live in Love with you.

The roots of womanhood live in you, our daughters. For you, we have sacred gardening to do. Songs. Ceremony. Self Love. Feed the root and you get a more beautiful flower. Feed the soul and you get a more beautiful light. Learning sacredness costs less than cosmetics, is more transformative, heals wounds lastingly, improves aging, rejuvenates more deeply, lasts longer, and blesses the world with true soul beauty that matters.

We aren't good at recognizing sacredness. This is a blindness. Sacredness is the truth inside every soul you meet. Sacredness is a habit. Practice with your every breath.

Hold us all responsible for your safety and wellness shine. Humanity will not fulfill its promise until womanhood is held sacredly. Until you no longer fear for your lives, nor spend life reclaiming your wholeness, gathering scattered dignities like shattered sea shells. Until you have no reason but to assume the flowering of your dreams. It should not ever occur to a girl that she is in jeopardy by birth, nor should she ever begin the sad burrowing into self betrayal. A tide of woman sacredness rises. That will be our new sun.

Sacred Love

All true Love is unconditional. How you feel about others need not get in the way of blessing yourself and the world with unconditional Love. Love doesn't care whether you feel someone is worthy of your Love. It's not your Love. Love is a wild thing, and free. It just wants to run through you unobstructed. It wants to flood your vessel and then flood the world. When you get out of the way, Love comes through you and soaks your soul and sorrows. Then it does the same to the world that touches you. Touch you first. With unconditional Love.

Unconditional Love is not *unconditional like*. Liking has nothing to do with Loving. Liking is a fickle approach-retreat, aversion-attraction. Love does not care about anything but Love.

If you spread enough Love soaked light wherever you go, eventually you begin to run into more and more Love, radiant and growing wildly. This is the bounty you reap. The most essential oil of all is Love. Sacred ointment for suffering. Salve for every soul. Sweet incense for all time.

Love is in the midst and mist of you. It pools in your pores. Pours from your eyes. Courses your blood rivers. Shivers with you in the cold. Lifts you in your sorrow. You do not have to wait for Love to arrive tomorrow. Love is with you.

Love will never stop etching its divine script into the ground of your fertile heart. Surrender everything you are to this clandestine composer. You were never meant to be dry notes on a page. You are music. A living thing. Fire.

Being a Lover has nothing to do
with having a Lover.

When you learn that you can have and give all the Love you ever wanted, without a relationship, you are free. You can be broken, perforated, or punctured and still absolutely gush with Love. On a wild spending spree of soulful wandering, you can be Love's fountain.

When you reach into clear water and take it in your hand, it begins to behave as to its nature. It flows out of your hand, back to itself. When you squeeze the water, wanting to keep it in your hand, it flows out quicker. Your grip chases it away. You lose it. Keeping your hand open, honoring your moment with the water, you create a holding space. The water pools in your palm. It stays. This, daughter, is peace. This is Love.

Today is for Loving. Yesterday, too. Same for tomorrow. Resist, and suffer. Surrender, and be free. Love is the most necessary human endeavor. Your entire nature is Love. All else is a tangent, an aimless drift.

Love is a beacon unto itself. When you Love more, more Love flocks to you. Love Loves Love. What we want most we already have. This is the quandary of being human. Fall in soulful Love countless times. Lose your heart boundary. Merge with infinite beauty.

There is no end to the beginning of Love. Open to its gift and it will open for you endlessly. If you want to be kissed by eternal sunlight, call yourself by your truest name: *Love*. Then live up to your name.

Love is a freedom, not a possessing. Be dawn for every soul. Behold how the rising sun touches living things. Touch like that. Inspire countless *soul-mances*.

Love's flower is always in bloom. Your heart wants that eternal beauty. If you open wide your divine heart, it can hold a sky full of Love. Even more than that. Every sunrise should have your soulrise. Wake like that. Make an offering. Put light into the world. Let sunrise be awed by your soulrise. Your light is infinite. Every day must have its sunrise. Every soul must have its sun.

Love is a silent scripture running through every heart. Decipher its meaning and you will grow quiet, too, for you will have become the wordless language that speaks perfectly for everyone. A tonic exists that cures and blesses everything: More Love. More Love. More Love.

When you open, spring's grace comes flooding in. When you close, a sea of blossoms crashes against your wall, creating a deep ache. Your heart wants its air, which is Love. Let the divine beauty in. Let it out. People will fear their own divine tenderness that you make them feel. Make them feel it.

Breathing Love is not like breathing air. The wider you open your heart, the more Love flows in, the more Love flows out. No contractions. If sacred Love wants to enter you, and this is your desire, open wide. For all that is not sacred Love, close the door.

Be very careful how you talk to yourself. It becomes your life. When I call you *BeLoved*, I am praying that you will choose to *be* Loved. By you. The world has always prepared for war, so it has always been at war. Being at Love takes preparation, softening of what is hard, opening what is closed. Prepare.

Daughter. Spend your life Loving.
Not seeking Love. Ocean need not seek water.

You are already water, precious daughter. You are whole. Live beautifully, as whole things do. If you chase Love, you will lose it. You can only have Love by being Love. It is a flame. You must be a flame. See how fire behaves with its heat. Then you will know how to be with Love.

Be so fragrant with Love that the honeybees will not leave you alone, and a million flower blossoms know your name. A flame lives in your soul that can give the whole world a fever. Make us sick.

The Love inside you is not for special occasions or special people. It is for every soul, every living thing, and every moment. Do not portion your most priceless gift. Give it all away and see it replenish itself infinitely.

Do not Love like a slave master Loves its slave: full of ego and entitlement, conditionally bound to satisfied servitude. Do not Love like a cage with teeth and claws clamping down on everyone you target. Do not Love fearfully. None of these are ways of Love. Strip the gripping away from your heart embrace. Learn to hold the way cloud holds sky. The way a note holds its song.

Forever grant freedom to what you Love, especially to your Lover. Though freedom is not yours to grant, grant it. Granting creates your way of seeing and being with those you Love. Daily granting opens your spirit and mind, kills off the poison of harmful expectation. Love the way seasons Love, bowing to each other, surrendering the floor, timely and with honor.

Love and emotional addiction are easy to confuse. Gentle yourself through. Love frees you into peace, returning you to your own soul over and again. Addiction tortures you with fearful possessiveness that can never be satisfied.

This is because you cannot own another soul, no matter how much you are addicted. Unless you are at peace with your own divine existence, you are not truly at peace. You deserve so much more than to live anxious and fearful. Authentic Love is not dependent. It is intimate. This difference means everything. Too many lose themselves in their fantastical quest to be saved forever by another. You are divine. You must not lose yourself. Nor do you have to. Plant yourself in Love's true garden. Purge yourself of a lifetime of false story seeds. Discover that you do not need to hold onto anyone to be okay. You were created for joy, which comes when you let go.

Notice how bees and butterflies visit only the flowers that are not grasping, squeezing, clenching. This is how Love cares to visit and pollinate your heart. Like a piano left out in the rain, you may need to tune your keys back to your original music. It can take time to learn how to be with yourself. Give the anxiety time to evaporate. The panic that feels like abandonment and free falling is the sensation of you returning to your soul. Once you arrive and acclimatize, take care to root yourself there. So you can truly Love: No emotional bondage. Only freedom between the safe flower you are and the beauty of what you Love.

Even a flower has the common sense to open when Love's sun comes calling. When Love in its endless variety and beauty speaks your name, say, *I am the one you are looking for.*

Some people say, *I Love you,* as though Love is a permission slip that allows them to bottle you up in a glass jar like a pet butterfly. We know how that ends for the butterfly. Don't be this kind of Lover. True Love is a freedom sky. What flies there flies freely. Love has never awakened in a mood to possess. When you are in this mood, you are not inside of Love.

Let your sweet soul uncurl its flower and show its divine heart to the world. Your fragrance is singular and should never be bottled or bound. Open and mist us wildly, you phenomenal dew.

Honey and poetry. That's what the whole world wants from you. Break open your heart hive. Set your sweetness free. Your Love is not a small fire in a big world. It is the world's entire light. Be our sunrise.

During your miraculous, precious, delicate time on this earth, pour out your Love. All of it. In every sweet moment granted you. Every soul you encounter dearly, secretly needs your Loving nectar. Every single drop.

Leave your Love song everywhere. Especially inside yourself. Your Love is a gift whose blessing you cannot fully know. Leave its divine pollen on everything, on moments, on hearts, on suffering. Let it birth dawns. Leave Love letters all over the world.

Love's ointment keeps your soul supple and fluid. Without Love, your soul is a riverbed without water. Sky without air. Life without beauty or grace. True Love is a freedom that touches everything with Creation song.

Life is an exercise in remaining open, *in spite of*. This is your Love rebellion, your grand art, your inheritance for the world. Protecting forests and oceans is vital. But if you do not learn how to protect your human heart, by honoring its river and sky nature, you cannot be well enough to protect the world. Being open does not mean to be available. It just means to be viable, supple, and pliant, a ready riverbed for your compassion.

———

A woman placed one hand on her heart, another on the sweetgrass. A current ran from the grass up into her. In that moment, she learned a new language. It healed her wounds. Revived her dreams. Made life radiant. She learned how Love speaks, began speaking that to her soul.

Loving Yourself

Daughter, I am going to tell you a secret: *You are the best thing that ever happened to you*. Love yourself this deeply. When you feel this and know this, you will be free.

Loving yourself is not selfish. Loving others without Loving yourself is not Love. It is a rootless desperation. A grasping. Your self is an intimate part of the world over which you have lifelong influence, a true foundation for nurturing the world. Loving yourself is not a competitive indulgence, a neglecting of others. Seeing life this way does not serve anyone, creates harm. When you Love yourself, you *are* Loving others, at your vital root.

Loving yourself is the seed. Unconditional Love is the flower. As you grow Love for yourself, you open your heart until it has the capacity for unconditional Love. The closer you are to feeling it, the less you suffer. The more you become medicine, the more the world heals.

You aren't here to be a part-time Lover. Your calling is to be wide open. To be that astounding light. As that light is for you, you can be for all. A journey not easy. Just worthy of your endurance. Your reward? A life of peace.

Just when you feel you are truly Loving yourself, another layer presents itself to you. Always go deeper. Does it nourish you? That is the question. Your wellness is a foundation for your free and beautiful life. Unwellness is a tyrant trying to force you to join it. Revolt. Live free and complete. Home sing your pieces. This is how peace is.

How well do you water yourself? What you deeply Love about yourself needs more Love. What you don't feel good about needs more Love. Shower all of you.

Do you grow your own soul food? Have your own garden for this, to feed your soul what it needs. Do not fall into dependence on external gurus, teachers, guides, counselors, and other people's life examples. Have a garden and grow close with it. Learn how to feed and water it, and the nature of what grows there.

She sent herself care packages,
and was delighted to receive every one.

Loving yourself is a culture. A language. A whole new world. It is the soil for every beautiful seed in your life. The bed that lifts your every blossom into being. Sink your whole life into Loving you. With such roots, you cannot be whittled away, reduced, bleached, dissolved, distorted, erased, silenced, or slaved. Root yourself.

Want yourself. Want yourself until your desire washes over your anxiety. No more yearning to belong. Only a boundless, breathing peace. Take passionate, wonderful, astounding care of you. As people pay attention to how beautifully you take care of you, you inspire them into the same beauty.

The voice that says you are not pretty enough, not funny, popular, liked, Loved, admired, respected, celebrated enough is not your voice. It is a cloud sent by old oppression to recruit you. Reject the invitation. A superior membership awaits you.

You are your soul's perfect medicine. Gift your true self to your true self. Oh how your life blooms when you finally believe in the truth of who you are. Sifting through the illusions and surface persona, you arrive at the miracle of you. The pure river made of Love. The sacredness that does not fear or despair, but simply flows, content and complete within itself. Taste that pristine water and never thirst or hunger again.

You ask, *How do I begin to truly Love myself?* Gently. With every thought, gently touch your feelings. Act, remember, and imagine tenderly. Clear your spirit of what is not Love. Be your own sanctuary.

Your heart, like desert earth, can grow hard and cracked without inner Love. Be a monsoon and shower yourself soft. If you water your softness, gardens will grow. If you water your tender places, you will bloom.

If you do not Love yourself, you are a hard ground unable to absorb the Love rain of others. The water washes away. Loving yourself softens your soil, for the seeds inside to get out as new life, and for the Love water to soak in. When you Love others but not yourself, you care for a field of flowers, but leave the soil unattended.

When you are alone at night in the forest, you build a fire. The fire keeps you warm and safe, lets you see through the darkness. Provides hope. This is what it means to Love yourself. Start and keep a fire. You have no need to shiver through the cold when you are a fire starter.

You cannot Love yourself too much, only falsely. When true, your Love bath need not end. Self Love is a continuous inner ovation, not a periodic smattering of applause. Not a part-time work, but a full-time calling. A rapturous gratitude, dissolving the self into Love's infinite ocean. A lifelong garden work. A passion project.

If you are going to splurge on anything, splurge on the way you Love yourself. Spend your time, your tears, your life. Spend everything. Stay up all night drinking your soul beauty. Intoxicated on your essence, dance on the bed, sing nonsense songs, jump with sunrise, run until your muscles and breath say, *This is the madness we have been waiting for.*

Your self Love work is not just for you. It is for all the generations of living things after you, blessed by your wellness and by the absence of your harmfulness. Your self Love is an inheritance for the world. Life untold will eat the fruit of your devotion.

She harvested her first crop of self Love.
It was the best feast of her entire life.

How self Love feels is nothing compared to the blessings it yields. Self Love can turn barrenness into a paradise, in your soul and in the world. Self Love births unconditional Love, that endless light of revival and hope.

Soulful nurturing is an art. You know better than anyone your favorite touches. Why wait for someone to gift you them when you can gift yourself? Not materialism. Soulfulness. Treating yourself is a habit. Many have become impoverished in the craft. Be creative. Select subtle sublime succulence. Life is precious. As are your joy and delight. Gift *you* wonderfully. For you are a gift.

Self Love is a priceless compass, map, and guide. Without self Love, you are deep underwater swimming for what you believe is the surface. Instead it is the bottom. Loving yourself orients you to the truth. Know your direction.

So many species are going extinct: *Integrity. Honor. Honesty. Nobility. Sacredness.* These living things have natural habitats you must protect. Landscapes like *Love, compassion, peace, stillness, wholeness, wellness.* Find out what makes your living things grow. Feed them that.

You know you have self Love when the story you tell yourself about yourself heals you. This world endlessly attempts to pull a woman away from herself and into its degrading idea of a woman. Go back to yourself. Go back home. Be with you. You need you.

If a bird spends all its time grounded, eventually it loses the ability to exist and function in the sky. Seeing each other's faces, hearing each other's voices, does more than fill our souls. It sharpens our instrument for seeing and hearing and feeling each other, and therefore ourselves. Soul time works the same way. Your ability to see, hear, feel, and comprehend your soul comes from spending time flying in it.

This world can erode girls, strip away their foundation of self Love. The act is gradual, can be inviting. One day, you naturally feed yourself what feels good to your soul. Another day, you find yourself as a woman so far out to sea you cannot see your soul. To be well as a woman is to choose continuous resistance to this subtle erosion. Persistent whole-keeping. Many want to break you down, fraction you up. Turn you into parts. Stay whole. Surround yourself with wholeness and whole-keepers. Make your freedom sing. You are everything.

The more you pour your care into others, the more you may lose track of pouring into yourself. If you are a caretaker for the world, you will be vulnerable to not caring for you. Stay in touch with the impulses and thoughts involved in your pleasing of others. This helps you stay close to the pleasuring of your soul.

Soul pleasure is unlike other pleasure. Soul pleasure nurtures you. Other pleasures can deplete you. Go back and look at your journey thus far. Did you begin to lose yourself at some point? What did you lose in the losing of yourself? What harm did you gain? You are not a fragile thing. Only your hurt is fragile. It is easy to confuse your hurt with your whole self. Your whole self is a mountain. A sky. A ceremony of generations.

Sometimes when you weep, you flood dry valleys with life-giving water. People will shame you into not flooding the world. Your flood may be what souls need most. A sky not afraid of crying is a sky at peace with itself, a sky of blessings. People use shame, guilt, and obligation to enslave you. Being attentive to these chains keeps you free. What is shame? A feeling that you have displeased others. Sometimes their displeasure is a sign you have Loved yourself.

If the names you call yourself are not a mantra that sings, how can you say you Love yourself? Loving you also requires giving things away. Letting things go. Washing things out. You could say your Love for you is a purging as much as a pouring. If you feel lighter after your personal rain, maybe it is because new things are growing, things composed of sky and laughter.

Self Love, and self respect and honor are not mythological ideas. They are your bedrock for a beautiful life. People who do not Love, respect, or honor your womanhood do not care that you live a beautiful life. They care most that you serve their idea of their own beautiful life. In the end, they devour themselves in the degradation of using. You cannot degrade another without degrading yourself. No exceptions exist to this. Men and women both have forever degraded womanhood. Now we are all degraded and seek desperately the way back home to wholeness.

If you take good care of you, you will feel well, live well, produce things that are well. If you take wonderful care of you, you will feel wonderfully, live wonderfully, and produce wonderful fruit. You are worthy of a wonderful life. Nothing can stop you from taking wonderful care. Instead of seeing this as an indulgence, you can see it as a completeness. Your life bursting at the seams with care.

Love yourself with a sweet ache. With sunrise labor. Love yourself silly. Seriously. Love yourself regardless. Not arrogantly. Not demeaning. That is not Love. Love sacredly. Polish your shine. Prepare your wings. Rain dance. Then Love what grows from the water. Oh, daughter. Stay you. And when you lose you, go and get you. Make Loving you your life.

Your soul wants to hear you sing your sacred song, an affirmation of your divine worth. And what are you worth? Everything. The nature of your soul is that it wants you to feel it entirely. When you don't, when you accumulate layers of false stories, you suffer. Peace is the soul saying, *It's good to have you home again. I've prepared your favorite dish: Unconditional Love.*

What does it mean to Love yourself? Is it the memory of peace in your cells, those tide pools holding your sacred stories? Maybe it is the gardening you do in your heart and mind, in the brevity between breaths. The stones you pull from your own soil. Or the intimate way you touch your own skin and soul, the paradise in that feeling, your lingering in that warm bathwater of reunion. How you recognize your essence in living things. The jewelry of your compassion you wear like ceremony. The ritual of covert romances with the jazz of your heartbeat, the sensuous tenor of your tenderness. The appraisal of your thoughts, those unprecedented patterns, artwork of consciousness in the mind's gallery.

Letting yourself smile at beauty and pain, that too is Love. And the wind on your cheek on a solar day. The vibration of birdsong in your marrow. To be composed. To exist. To be a riverbed vulnerable to the flood. The taste of soul water. Gathering homegrown wildflowers from the meadows of your inner life. The scent of becoming. The copper tang of relationship. And when you choose to be alive, achieving joy's sensation. The holiness you are, created thing. Worship. Repair. Pulse. Noticing a moment. Being with it. Donating your entire being. Yes, daughter, this could be you. In Love.

Your Freedom

Why live your life as though you are a patch of air when you are the entire sky? You are a continent. Don't live like a crumb. Be boundless. Don't shrink. Bloom. Don't ask. You exist. That is your permission.

Freedom is acquainted with pain. It bleeds. It knows remorse and fear. These things do not own freedom. Freedom is free. Freedom is not owned by anyone. Not by any way, belief, or pot of worldly wealth. It does not scorn ideology or nation. It simply does not care about their existence, for freedom is free.

We want freedom, so we pursue it with the same ownership spirit and mind we have used in life. We go after freedom with ropes and chains and cages. We never catch freedom this way. Freedom cannot be caught, bought, or bartered. We cannot take a class or get a degree in freedom of the soul. Good deeds do not guarantee freedom. Freedom is not a bounty, and we need not be hunters.

Daughter, because many do not want you free, align yourself with those who do. Learn their ways. Evolve your own freedom language together. Build freedom ways. Heal together. Healing is a womb where freedom gestates. Purge your spirits of what is not free. This means people, places, ways, and stories. Be careful of stories. They can be spirits that incarcerate. Stories can be caravans of cages and dungeons whose words are contracts that render you indentured.

Pay attention to stories people bring you about what it means to be or not be a woman. How you violate womanhood, or what you should aspire to as a woman. Watch these stories. Listen. Discern their finer threads and the needles that wove them.

Freedom is not as much disobedience as it is obedience to your wondrous soul. If you are told to be quiet, sing. If you are told to sit, stand. Fall back? Step forward. Shrink? Expand. Find the sky of your being today. Soar joyfully.

Your freedom is in your language. If you do not understand, perhaps you have not had your language erased. If you have, may you grow a thousand tongues of freedom. If you want to speak freedom, you cannot use slave language. If you use slave language, you wake the slave in you.

Stay sky. Don't shrink, burrow, hide, succumb. Stay mountain. Stay ocean, river, rumble, legend. This takes deep gardening, daily persistent knees in the soil, dirt under your nails. The sweat of preservation, of staying in tune. You are a perfect instrument. Life is playing its miracle through you. Dilate, soften, soak, stretch. Resist.

Take note of the exponential to your potential. Gaze your universe, your potency, your scale: canyon grand, grand grain of the finest sand, always grand even in your subtlety, your humility. Bow before divinity, but nothing else. Stand before what wants you small. Speak in the face of what wants you silent. Some want to see you in fractions and fragments, in possessive convenience.

When you encounter those who want you as an offering to their idea of woman, burn down their entire altar with your truth. Truth need not be violent, though it is direct. If you find someone dumping pollution into your pristine river, rise up in your truth and flood that moment's valley. Birth your wholeness repeatedly.

If you find this exhausting, know that your erosion into parts and pieces is a worse exhaustion. It tires your soul until your soul wants nothing but to lie down and be run over, to be discarded into the mouths that keep coming for your willingness. If you can find a way not to be willing, you will have willed a revolution. Then watch the false warriors flee into the woods of their failure. Watch them, feeling not glee but the high tide of evidence: *This is what happens when you remain a whole human being.*

In a world that persists in your enslavement, always be freeing yourself. Every thought. Every beat of your drum. Don't just rock the boat. Sink it and learn to swim. Always move toward freedom. One day the lost ghosts will realize no one can own the earth, nations are imaginary castles with imaginary moats, and souls are free.

Love freedom more than you Love ease. Love it enough to wring it from your soul, like sky summoning its sweet rain. Drench your life in permission. Vacate your fear. Breathe a revolutionary breath.

Preserve yourself. Don't go extinct. You are precious water. Share yourself consciously. Sharing is sacred. Giving to what only wants to take is desecration. Your life deserves more than that. Burn shame, guilt, and obligation in the fire of self Love. Sacredly share your body, brilliance, support, time, energy, investment, and care. Share because your soul desires it. Your wellness need not be an endangered species.

So many live shackled and caged. Fear is the warden and the steel. Recognize the ways you are not living free. Give yourself permission to be free. Do the lifelong work of learning to be free. Freedom is not an entitlement. It is a consequence of resisting what would enslave you. It is a song you sing to keep you close to your true nature and calling. A fruitfulness of the soul worthy of your impassioned labor and continuous revolt.

Freedom is a sky beyond the sky. Just when you believe you have reached it, you discover more atmospheres to pierce. Freedom is an endless unveiling, a continuous movement through a bright billowing of sheers. If you feel you have tasted freedom, know that you have tasted but a particle of a crumb of a crust of an infinite baking. An immeasurable dissolution. An evaporation timeless and profoundly worth your lifelong endeavor.

Freedom is a choice before it is a condition. Not self determination, but soul-determination that washes the self into union, into harmony with all things. Freedom does not oppress. It frees. Destroy all your soul cages. Set the wild things in you free.

Sometimes you may fight against being owned, by owning yourself. Now you are your own oppressor. No life can be owned. No soul is inherently slave. Allow your spirit to use its wings. Your nature is freedom. Do not be yet another slave master to your own being. You live in a world of slaves and slave masters, everyone practicing ownership. The social pressure is immense, contagious. Be on the lookout for ways you cage yourself. Be a devoted breaker of cages.

Go back to the moment of your birth. Promise yourself: *No more illusions*. Experience truth. Don't be a slave to the dream others are living. How this will shape you, no one can know. Knowing is not the point. Freedom is.

Woman. No greater oppression has been. No greater revolution shall be. Many ways exist to lead a revolution. Start by overthrowing your fears. For the revolution ahead, we call for Lovers. If they try to enslave, oppress, and dehumanize you, you must be a powerful thing. Nobody takes the time to hold down what they think can never rise up. You are tribal. Do not stop dancing. This is how you stay you, how you stay in this world, not a ghost, but a living thing.

What are the words you use to resist oppression? If you do not have your own reliable, lush library, you will come up mute when you need affirmation the most. *I will not be reduced*. These words are strong medicine. You can use them anytime someone attempts to take your power, fails to see you, corrals you into a narrow canyon of prejudiced idea. *I will not be reduced*. A good tonic against fear and bullying. Against slave masters and sickened souls who struggle with your version of womanhood. And when you are clenched by doubt, you have your response: *I will not be reduced*.

She practiced Loving herself until her
self became Love. At last, she was free.

To study freedom, behave like the sky. When your self dissolves into all things, all things are now your self. In this state, no fear exists. No impulse for protection. Your existence is no longer a timid traveler in a sea of Creation. It is Creation itself. To take such a divine breath of being, to at last dilate into the full bloom of your boundless soul, is surely freedom.

Do not let your life be a continuous apology. You have the same right as a mountain or the sky to take up space. To exist. To assert your personal testimony. Do not shrink or hide. Be an entire, liberated life.

Women looked at each other with new fire, which was very old. The ancient one cried. Birds hushed. The valley of souls felt all of this and knew its scent. They had birthed it.

Wholeness

Have you devoted time defining what it means for you to be whole? Do you have a clear sense of what this looks, feels, acts like? The greater your clarity, the more you empower yourself to enter the atmosphere of wholeness, and to remain there. If you define wholeness according to how others define it, you will manifest their idea of wholeness, not your own actual wholeness. Knowing your wholeness takes courage and a willingness to think and feel for yourself.

Thinking and feeling for ourselves is hard. We take it for granted. Mostly, we live out communal agreements. Each of us has different points of tolerance for diverging from the herd. Some stay close to the center of the herd for a lifetime, filled with fear and insecurity or just a natural need to be at the center.

Others find their peace at the edge of the herd. Some flee the herd entirely, running for their lives to the hills where they may or may not contribute to the herd in some way. What is your conformity setting? This relates to how you define wholeness. True wholeness has something to do with the herd and a great deal to do with your unique soul settings.

She decided she was enough.
Everything changed.

You are not anyone's appendage. Your soul belongs at the center of your life, with all else orbiting. You are free to occupy your whole self. Living life quarantined within a narrow, devalued identity is a waste of life and blessings. Like living on a single rock when you have the whole mountain. You deserve to enjoy all your soulful acres. The world needs all your gifts.

Practice seeing yourself without boundaries. If in your vision you see signs that say *No Trespassing*, take them down and run out to meet the rest of yourself. You are a miracle with which you ought to be fully acquainted. Travel your sacred land.

You aren't fruit to be picked. You are the orchard. Live abundantly. You are earth. Water. Wind. Sun. Seeds. Roots.

Living whole is an art when your kind has been taught to live in parts. Bless you. You are forever ripening.

You are an entire life. All by your sacred self. Live richly in your relationships. Live even more richly in yourself. You were born a completed thing. Loving yourself means knowing this. The people in your life do not complete you. They reflect you. And you them. Be Loving mirrors for each other. Reveal one another. Remain whole. That's your revolution.

Spiritual Life

The ancient one's eyes teared as he spoke:

It is morning now. I hear this ocean of birds. How they have waited the night, faithfully, for this offering of sun. What living things do when the sun rises and sets is the purest praise and worship I know.

All true life is spiritual life. Separating the spiritual from the not-spiritual is an exercise in blindness and sleepwalking. *Not-spiritual* does not exist. How you clean your teeth is spiritual. If you ever lose your teeth, you will sing praise at the chance to have teeth to clean again. Anything that awakens your bond with all things is a spiritual blessing.

All living things are living a spiritual life, in chosen or forced communion with Creation. Every soul has faith. Faith in its fear, hate, kindness. Faith in something. We cannot live without faith. Your faith makes your journey.

Spiritual practices alone don't make you pure. Only Love can do that. Souls don't fall apart. You do, when you live as though you are not soul. And what is soul? Your soul is an ocean. Your spirit, the mist rising there.

My soul is my monastery.
Peace the garden I grow.

Faith fires up freedom, which waits in the simmering embers of your soul desire for its sweet day. Faith and hope are kindling for the fire of living. Run wild dealing out hope. Give it away to everyone. Don't charge a price. Let your faith swell in you until it bursts out and soaks whoever comes near. Love is a sanctuary. Portable, and always available for use. As is hope. When the flood comes, hold on to your hope. It will keep you afloat.

Sun. Sky. Breeze. Trees. Water.
These are my sanctuary and sermon.
Their serenity performs my prayer.

If you seek spiritual guidance, seek from the source, or close to it. If you drink from diluted water poured by one who knows only how to imitate deeper teaching and living, you will miss the water's original minerals. If you want to chew a bone, see if it still has its marrow.

A spiritual life is a practice in grace. Learning to see, feel, receive, share, and live in grace. With these soft breaths and tender touches you gather grace, sweet grace. You are the location of your spiritual life. Be the praise and worship.

Protect your spirit, the energy you are filled with and exude. It determines your life. Don't let others pollute or bring your spirit down. By nature, you are weightless, breezy, a clear stream running. Nothing you have matters if you don't have harmony with your spirit. It can keep you afloat, insulate you from social harm. Avoiding conflict is a strategy. But a pure spirit is life.

Spend time in your intimacy with all things. Feel those things on your skin like mist, in your heart as a verdant patch of clover. Taste your relations. Listen. Teachings come through always. *Touch*. With your sensitivity. Your discernment. Your instinct.

Relationship is your wealth: *Creator. Created. Creation.* Feel all of this at once in your soul and cells. Stay soaked in this rain, rested in this darkness, alive in this light.

What is prayer? When your soul behaves like an eagle in the wind. Remember, you are a living prayer. Feeling empty? Be prayer full. A day is a prayer. Your eager concentration in a moment of discovery is prayer, too: a reaching out to all that is to join with truth. Art and science live in every soul.

When you open a window, this, too, is a prayer. You are asking fresh air to enter and bless your life. And you give thanks for the fresh air to come. When you open windows in the heart, soul, mind, body, you enter prayer. How can you believe in the power of thinking and not believe in the power of praying? A prayer is a thought soaked in soul.

Spend your life opening these soul windows and your days will be rich with meaning and beauty and reason. Let life's rivers run freely through you, through your prayer. If you pray like a child asking for a birthday gift, with selfish wanting dripping from your words, you may not like what you receive. Pray like a gull in the sky exuding its joy at flight. Pray like flames climbing each other to reach the moon. Pray every living thing into your soul, an invitation to jump in and rejoice with you. Pray yourself back to yourself. Pray your Love across distance and into lives and moments. Pray a quilt of compassion.

Your touch can be a prayer. Your tears. Brushing your skin against the coat of an animal. Nuzzling a flower blossom in your palm. Sipping from a stream. Move through your moments prayerfully and life slows. Calm spreads in you. You regain your natural rhythm and breath and heartbeat. And when you look at yourself and think of yourself, do it prayerfully. Not asking. Marveling. Seeing the awesome soul of your life.

Your prayer life is much more than words. It shines in every dimension, a living grace. When you are weary or in dire need, pray deeper. Sincerity births miracles.

Be careful not to fall too far into the well of your ideas. Your beliefs can be like a bright wind carrying you up into your truth. They can also be a staircase leading you into a dungeon of frightened conviction.

If you let others determine for you where your God is located, how to access your God, the word and meaning of your God, the nature of Godliness, or the existence of God, then your God will not be your God. Your God will be another person's idea of God. If you want your own God, dare to have your own divine experience.

Let your soul decide your faith. If your soul leads you to the most conventional religious life, be devoted to that doctrine. If your soul leads you to chase butterflies on a mountaintop, be devoted to that wordless scripture.

Do not let others bully you into using their religious language. Holiness and you have your own sacred words and ways. You have the right to give your God, your grace, endless names. No human laws or judgments matter in this. Let others fret about following group instructions. Strip off your conformity clothes and laugh and cry and sing and dance and silence yourself into glory. What sweet unknowable privacy, your soul and Soul.

The size of the congregation around you is not affirmation you are on the right path. Millions of souls will follow each other to doom and destruction. A single hummingbird can remind you of the grace of joy. Numbers are not your security blanket. Nor is the volume of the preaching, or the shine of the clothes. Only your soul can know. Only your soul.

If you are swimming in the ocean, is it more meaningful for you to believe in the ocean or to experience the ocean? And if you are immersed in God, Creator, Divine, is it more meaningful for you to believe in that holiness or to experience it? Humans use beliefs as weapons in ego combat. But if you truly experience what is sacred, it can free you from the illusion that belief is greater than truth. Spend your life soaked in truth. Speak, exude, see, seed, hear, act, feel, reflect, inspire, illuminate, reflect truth.

Soul power dwarfs solar power and makes summer feel like a drop of warmth, a sliver of light. If you knew how powerful your soul is, you would create the life of your dreams and fill the world with your soulfulness. It is in our not knowing that we shrink and yield. Know your power. Grow your power. Sow your power.

As you are a soulful thing, it is necessary that you live soulfully. When you do not, you suffer. Suffering is a divine reminder: *Return to your nature.*

Dearly thirsting for holiness, we mark people as saints, and places as sacred. But holiness is all around and within us. Behold the unfortunate human miracle: We have found a way to be inside an endless lake of holiness and not get wet.

Your yearning is a crumb from the bread of holiness. Surrender. Taste every grain. Your feast may be found inside your faith. Grace is everywhere. Look.

Have you heard the voice of God? Then you know all language is a yearning translation of Love. Some say no one has ever heard the voice of God. They must not know the sound of sky rumble, of a lioness purring with her litter, water vibrating on a blade of grass, or a thought soaked in Love.

Your spiritual life can be a powerful anchor, reminding you that you are real, worthy, irrevocably complete. Nothing is required of you to join the club of belonging. Your spiritual life needs your gentle attention—the soil, water, and sunlight that makes it grow. Practice diving beneath the surface in every moment. Whatever you touch, feel. Whatever you see, see into. Dive deeper into whatever you notice. A richer meaning and grace await.

Learn to see what you are not accustomed to seeing. The people in your life are not here because you have stumbled upon them. Look more deeply into who they are, what they are to you, and how they stir your waters. If they don't stir your waters at all, ask a question from the heart of your spiritual life: *Am I passively allowing them to occupy my life, or am I actively keeping them present for no purpose?* Purpose is a diviner. You can look into it and see what needs to stay and what needs to go. Purpose forever whispers the season of your life.

If your faith does not pull you into Love but sweeps you into being hurtful, question your faith. Question your way of being in your faith. Don't use your suffering to shape your faith into a weapon. Surrender your suffering into your forge of forgetfulness, that it may be transformed into a kindness. Your faith can swell your ego. Maybe this is not faith but fear. If your faith leaves you dissolved into Creation, see what it feels like to stay and live there.

Take trips away from this world as often as you can, to the place where your soul goes to dream. Come back glistening with that mystic dew, wild and new.

She prayed. Then she believed.
Then she achieved. That's how she did it.

When you decide to become a soul beautician, your appointment book will overflow with light. We need more soul salons. Soul gardens. Soul cafes. Soul music. Civic soul beautification projects. Sculpt your soul. Let it reveal your truest form and nature.

Many of our systems that exist to nurture wounded souls end up wounding them further. This is not because of an absence of knowledge. It is because of an absence of soulfulness, which breeds the presence of unwellness in healers themselves. Sing psalms down by the river of your soulfulness. Sing a rapturous song until all that weighs on you, like a startled flock, gets up and leaves.

You ever notice how some people, when you first meet, are in a rush to prove their spiritual enlightenment to you? That's okay. Give them a hug and call them *Guru*.

If you can learn to live in a state of worship, of abiding Love for your life and its moments, your heart will grow tender, birthing a new ease in you. Every day is a sermon, and the sermon is Love.

Soul stirs wonderfully and childlike as the sun rises. Imagine what the world does as your soul rises. Please, give us that gift. Even if you don't ever see the evidence, you will have brought a multitude of wonders to life.

When you stay in your purpose, you fill with a sense of nobility, of meaningful duty and service. Do not think so little of your presence in the world that you miss your calling. Life is your ordination. Living is your ministry. Love your greatest psalm.

It is enough to be the quiet wind in the valley,
unseen, that moves through every living thing.

Even when it is not fashionable, be humble. Especially then. Humility invites the light of grace to work in your life. Humility is evidence of your spiritual life. When you see how large and near and woven together everything is, you see your true place. Not oversized or undersized. Not irrelevant or superior. A part of it all. Enough.

Humility is not a mask you wear. It is your true face, not an act for appearance's sake. It is your private truth diffusing fragrance publicly. Bow down and be lifted. Keep your knees in the earth and your life will be elevated. Be humbled by everything. Every single blessed thing.

Ceremonial Life

You need ceremonies to stay in your sacredness. Without ceremonies, you leave your door open and they will steal you from yourself. Who are *they*? Anyone who would do such a thing. Ceremonies keep you close to your soul fire, illuminating truth and chasing illusion away.

To be sovereign is to exist of your own accord, within your own authority and autonomy. To have freedom. Cedar, sweetgrass, sage, tobacco, you—sacred, sovereign things. Smudge yourself in what is pure, to enter purity and become a vessel for what is pure.

Hard times call for softness. Soul. Ceremony. Song. Surrender. Place your hand over your womb place. Breathe Lovingly. Say these things: *Grace, glory, ground. Wind, warrior, wound, woman. Freedom, fierce, fire, found. Night, nectar, new, now. Sanctuary, sacred, sun. Drum, dance, delirious. Ceremony, celebrate. Birth, become, born.* Say these things.

Ceremonies cleanse you. We often confuse our heart for a trashcan instead of the sacred space it is. Everything has its place. Garbage doesn't belong in the heart. Only Love ceremonies do. Burn, birth, baptize, become.

Feel all of it. Embrace your divine greatness, your sacred splendor. Be your own ceremony. Dance and sing through night and dream till dawn has come and gone. Make good medicine with your holy life.

Your soul is a smoke lodge. Lay down your cedar, smudge yourself, enter, and pray. Stay there. Over and again, sing and dance self Love. Sacredness. Preservation Song. Keep weaving yourself back together, daughter. Use sweetgrass, sweet nectar, anything good for repairing your sweet soul.

––––––––

She opened her heart and called to her water, saying, *I am the power of ocean. Irrevocable tide in the marrow of moon. Say peace when you come to me. For I swallow the bones of outcast Love, walk sacredness back into the world. Breathing praise.*

Womanhood

When I call you *woman*, I am not calling you only woman. I am not casting nets, pile-driving steel bars for your captivity. I am not saying what you are or what you are not. No. When I call you woman, I am singing. I am praying. I am calling out glory in its deepest name. When I call you woman I am beholding. Reminding. Kneeling. Praising. When I call you woman I send streams of you through my forest, clearing the underbrush, startling the birds into song. I am peering into God and catching your effervescence.

When I call you woman I speak a ceremony with no finality. This I call you is a healing lodge, smoke burst sent out to diffuse mundane neighborhoods with wilderness. When I call you woman, I call for sacredness. Might. Memory. Able-ness, that sable nest that is the beginning of flight and sky. Womanhood is yours, not mine, not anyone's. My words are but Love's gushing. I am grateful to have you consider what spirit says through me:

If you fall too deeply into your identity as woman, things may fall into that well with you, dust from other people's definition of a woman. Fall deeply into your identity as a soul, arrive at your own pure idea of a woman.

If you try too hard to reject the stereotypes and stigmas piled onto girls and women, you may become those things. Or you may become the opposite of them, which can be just as harmful, to you and others. If you fight stereotypes, those ideas will engage with you intimately and enter you. Instead of fighting, of proving otherwise, of sprinting in the opposite direction, settle into the sacred lake that is your soul. Settle into being you, whatever that confirms or disconfirms about stereotypes. Settle into your truth, a living peace.

You cannot control how others perceive you. That is their journey. Release your hold on it. Their journey is a powerful kite that will sweep you into the far sky and away from yourself if you do not let go of the kite string. Let go and sink down into your warm bath of soulfulness. Bathe in your own waters. This is your revolt against stereotypes, to not be consumed with them. To feel your bath soften and enter you.

You may feel a constant, heavy rain over your life. An expectation that as a girl or woman you remain pure. Love yourself by looking deeply into this idea. What does it mean for you to be pure? Group ideas of purity are not always worth your consideration. Consider your life and purity, for your sake. How do you walk with it? Maybe you kick it to the roadside, or hold it closely in your arms. Find your own purity. Decide its place in your life.

What are the code words used to hold you down? Lift them up into the light of your caring attention. What do they mean to you? If their spirit assaults your womanhood, your personhood, get rid of the words. Change their meaning for you, if you wish. Be aware that they can still carry residue and sediment of their original meaning. Freedom wants its own special language.

It is hard work to examine the true meaning of being woman in a culture constantly burying you in its own ideas. How much bleeding are you willing to endure to remember the original truth of being woman, before the burying began? Until this world changes, for you to Love yourself, you are required to excavate constantly. You are at the bottom of a deep sand pit. Culture is a monstrous shovel tossing sand on top of your womanhood. To keep your head above the sand, it is not enough to periodically examine your identity. Sweep the sand away with every thought and breath.

Your River Nature

Yours is a story of water. All the oceans, seas, rivers, rain, and lakes you have ever known are only mirror images of the mystic flow within you. How is your water? Your tears are salt and soul. Song and soil. Let your sweet river run. Cry sometimes. Give honor to the water you are.

Please do not apply a tourniquet to the bleeding that revives your soul. Everything in you is designed to flow. Set your rivers free. Supple your way forward. River like. Your reservoir is much deeper than you believe. Drink. You are Love's fountain. Flood the world.

They told her not to be emotional.
So she released her ocean
and blessed all living things.

Living things must be watered. That's what your tears are for. Keep your ground soft and your river flowing. Don't

43

cry in. Cry out. Crying in, you flood yourself and drown. Crying out, you water souls with your tender song. After you weep, your soul, your soil, is soft. This is a good time to plant healing seeds.

Day is a river. If you soak yourself in it, day will wash your spirit clean. You and day will be two flowing waters, a harmony. Stay in your spirit. Life flows easier this way. Like mountain spring water trembling and bright from birth, flows the purity of your heart. Breathe and grow calm. If you slow your river, more light can dance in it.

If they tell you that you are a dam, a hard, cold barrier to the flow of life, do not believe them. Keep on rivering. They will say your tears are a shameful thing and should be hidden. Your tears are the ocean that is your soul, a great water to wash the world clean. Bring them. If you have lakes of tears inside, water somebody's drought-struck life. Use your feelings.

Sweet soul, even your sadness is a precious season, an alchemy. And your sunbreak after, the light that spills like butter on newborn ground. Look at willow trees after rain. Even they know that when blessed with what life offers, it is good to weep.

Your soul is a vast and wondrous river. Don't treat it like a puddle of mud. It asks you to flow. Please, let go. River yourself home to peace. What you water grows. Especially your own soul. Monsoon yourself. Do river things daily.

Your Body

Your body is not your body in the way that people possess animals they call pets, or children they raise, or land they presume to purchase. Your body is your body in the way sun is sunlight's body. No ownership exists. No judgment.

No mutilation or fear. Just a free existence of sunlight inside of sun. Of sun inside of sunlight. A peace of being. Your body is your body in this way. It is a duty you have toward the carriage of your soul.

Your body performs millions of miracles daily. It is the greatest healer and artwork you will ever know. It is worthy of your Love. My heart breaks when you misunderstand your body, desperately trying to control it through contortion, shame, pride, or abandonment. Your body is not a wildness to tame. It is yours to exist with, to marvel at, to garden and learn. It is not your possession. It is a burst of light, temporal and phenomenal, in your rich array of illumination.

Your body is your body. What you do with it is your sovereign right. You are a sovereign land. Your *reasons* for what you do with your body are roots that create your happiness, sadness, peace, and despair. What are your deepest impulses? When you show off your body for attention, this is not liberation, freedom, or empowerment. It is enslavement to attention, which is a fickle reward. Attention, money, social rewards—if these are roots for what you do with your body, know that such roots bear barren fruit. Each time you depend on such external things and receive them, you weaken your bond with your soul. You lose your inward Love.

Do you Love other people's bodies more than your own? This is a recipe for suffering. It is possible for you to Love your body more, even if you feel far away from that. Cherishing yourself, any aspect of yourself, is innately built into you. A survival component. Cherishing is a form of Love, a pure valuing and longing. If you don't feel this, it is because the feeling has been muted or short-circuited. By your living. This also means that your living can return you to a full, active Loving of your body.

When you reject your body and its features, you reject your own soul. You reject your ancestral inheritance. You reject life's idea of your beauty. Do not let the world's sickness become your own. Your skin is not your sin. Not Loving it is. Your shape is not a failure. It is a wonder, an endless dance. Your features and functions are for living, not for criticizing, hiding, regretting. Gently remove these sicknesses from your being. Return to bloom.

No matter how much melanin you are dwelling in, it means everything that you bathe in your glory. Love your skin. It is not just a covering. It is the organ that cradles you. See how it Loves you? You cannot Love you without Loving your cradle, your signifier of your ancestors, and the divine work of sunlight and shadow.

At what age does a young girl go from presenting her smile to the world to presenting her body parts? What does this change mean? Who benefits? Social attention may feel good. But if it is just another fix in your addiction, it sickens you. How the world values you and its perception of your parts matters not nearly as much as how you value your whole, and the rejection of being parted. You are not body parts. You are a whole divinity. Live an indivisible, entire life.

Every morning, she stood at the mirror
and praised every part of her body.
Her body didn't change. She did.

Desire for attention is not superficial. It comes from the soul. Our great confusion is that we believe this desire is fulfilled by using our bodies, by seducing. The soul's desire for attention cannot be quenched this way, for its actual desire is for attention from *itself*. Showing off your body for attention brings attention that does not feed the soul, but instead leaves the soul empty and yearning all the more. It is your sovereignty to do what you will with your body. Your soul flowers when this doing is driven by a profoundly private Love for yourself, a gardening no one else need ever know.

All your life the world has told you your worth lives in your body, your face, your hair. You see how slavery works? If they can get you to believe the lie of your value-location, they can make money from you. And pleasure and power and control. In this spirit, they cannot make Love from you. Only you can do that. Your worth lives in your soul, radiates out through your being, and touches everything. If you spend your life chasing your worth in your appearance, you will always be chasing. If you spend your life immersed in the worth of your soul, you will have freedom from the chase.

Your womb is not a physical location. It is a spirit-power concentrated in part of your body and running through your being. Honor your womb. It is the most awesome creative force in this world. Birth is not its only function. It is a clock on earth keeping time with the heavens. A timepiece orchestrating your dance with moon and sun. Your womb is a garden harboring all your sacred cycles. When you are not in touch with your womb, humanity is not in touch with itself. We are sent spinning off our axis, lost from our equilibrium. Wars happen when woman is not at the center of keeping peace. Not because woman is more peaceful. But because balance is a root of peace, and your womb, both physical and spiritual, is an instrument of balance.

If your shape suddenly turned into that of a bullfrog, would you mourn your old shape? Maybe you would begin wanting to be shaped like a better bullfrog—a new season of suffering. Your shape will always be an enigma. No one can possibly understand it. Including you. But what to do with this enigma? You could be in despair. Or you could laugh. Value ease, not the disease of *dis-ease*.

To dissolve the distorting, devaluing, dehumanizing, objectifying, prostituting, self rejecting seeds about your body planted in you over a lifetime, take a thousand spoonsful daily of these words: *My body is sacred. I am sacred. I honor my sacred things.* Wash the words down with spring water, lemon water, tears. At first, the words may taste foreign, bitter, unwanted. Soon your self hating taste buds will die. Self Loving taste buds will bloom. Your life will change. It will become something that feels, thinks, acts, creates, rejoices. Sacredly.

Your body is the architecture of your every ancestor. Behold your generations. No more looking for flaws. Bow down. Your shape and contours have been perfected over thousands of years. Praise your land.

Body Love is fruit from the tree of self Love. Vintage wine has nothing on you. Your vintage is measured in millennia. Bow down and cherish all of you.

> *When her yearning to reveal her soul*
> *became greater than her yearning*
> *to reveal her body, she was free.*

As often as sunrise, honestly examine your desires, and how they relate to how you treat yourself. Clarify whether your desires are actually native to your soul, and not fed into you by a world that wants to devour you. If you use your body as bait, it is likely to draw piranhas. If you treat it as an altar, you can expect sacredness to arrive.

Your Appearance

People have obsessed over your appearance, always. I pray you do not join them in this obsession. If this is the bottomless abyss into which you fall as you relate to yourself, what tragedy. It would be the beginning of your soul starvation, your neglect of serving unconditional self Love on your daily plate.

Too many gravestones might accurately read: *Here lies a person. She spent her life obsessing over her appearance.* Or, *He never stopped looking in the mirror.* With each so-called compliment you have received since birth, you have been basted for the grill. Each time further readied to be eaten, objectified, consumed. Consumed as a product, consumed for your fear of not looking beautiful.

Can you feel, since your birth, your tribe's desperate need to call you beautiful? They are desperate to feel beautiful themselves. You are the offering their misplaced need is spilled into. You *must* be beautiful. You *have to be*. Or else what will become of them? Of you?

This rain of compliments does not serve you. It imprisons you. If you grow addicted to sabotaging affirmations, what becomes of you when the compliments end? Too many people know the answer, for they have been such addicts, and have met the unavoidable drought. Do not let yourself be identity-fattened for slaughter, daughter. Do not become the razor-narrow-identified thing of *beauty* many want you to be.

Being called beautiful does not make you secure in your appearance. Just the opposite. The constant label creates a pressure to meet an expectation, a monstrous fear that tomorrow, or someday, no one will call you beautiful anymore. It is possible to compliment someone to death. The word *beauty* can become a weapon of entrapment, a soul toxin, when it is used to the exclusion of recognizing, honoring, and activating all of a person.

People told her she should be a model.
So she modeled self Love.

Many people want to affirm themselves vicariously through you. They say, *Use it before you lose it. If you got it, flaunt it. Work it, girl.* These people may Love you deeply. Please do not confuse their confusion with their Love for you.

People capitalize on your appearance-insecurity. They make billions from your rejection of yourself, your microscopic assessment of flaw and imperfection. They eat your soul. They eat your money. They eat your peace. They eat your relationships, leaving you lonelier, more needful, more of an offering to their appetite. They serve you up to the masses whom they have prepared to feast on you. Masses conditioned to have a taste for you, a taste for desperation, depression, and despair.

Do not let yourself be basted in compliments that erode your wholeness. Don't jump on the grill to be liked, befriended, followed, fawned over, erected as a soulless model, only to have the crowd then tear you down. When they say, *You should be a model*, take the opportunity to go wild. Respond, *A model of what? Astro-physical dynamics? Self loathing? Self Love? Self honor? Dignity? Peace? Kindness? Please specify, so I may know how you see me. Or rather, how much of me you see.*

You see, I am a glorious, deep ocean. I carry more fathoms than you can fathom. Where you believe you have reached the final depth of me, I am just beginning. In your mind, you keep reducing me to surface spray. In my mind, I will keep building myself up into the everything I am and am to be. With my speech and walk and thought and touch, I aim to make my ancient grandmothers smile. With my heart and soul and genius, I intend to make my ancient grandfathers bow down in pride and honor for what I choose to be.

So, yes, I am a model. I model the all-ness of womanhood. I model exemplification of being human. I do not aspire to be equal to man. I am equal to all things. I aspire to be faithful to me. I model resistance to your reduction of me. Resistance to all ideas of woman that turn me from a kaleidoscope of dimensions into a helpless thing to be used, bruised, denounced. I am announced. I am a model for majesty. For integrity. For imperfection and flaw. I am a model for the raw, the becoming, the growing, the pain and its showing.

I model Love that puts fears to rest. I model bravery and warriorhood, that fierce spirit of life protection. I model self correction. Peace inflection. Resurrection of what centuries have put asunder. I am not blunder, departed from man. I am that I am. I model full throttle freedom made woman. Woman, I stand. Woman, I sing. Woman, I bring up to my surface and convey a thing children can look to and see: This womaning is a sacred thing.

You are most glorious liberated from worry over your appearance. This is possible even as you enjoy your outer beauty. You can breathe beautifully and not be self conscious of your breathing. Same with your thinking, creating, caring. You can look beautiful in whatever way beautiful means to you and still not be drowned in your looks. You can stay stable and upright on the shores of your wholeness. You can swim in all your waters, joyfully.

Daughter, when you look at your face in the mirror, you behold the faces of your ancestors. The sum of their song and sojourn. May you never again find fault in it.

From birth you will be referred to by your appearance. This is why you must spend your life Loving your soul. Love your soul. Love it. The unseen part of you is real, a wilderness that needs your Love. Your Love affair with your body is personal work, not public property. Remember that.

You are not an ornament.
Don't leave yourself hanging.

Every time someone focuses on your appearance, don't let this detach you from your innerness. In a world fixated on your form, Loving your soul is a rebellion into wholeness. Model that. Show how you show up for you. Inspire a soul movement. You are the center of your life, not a passive rock orbiting someone else's life. Your life is a mystic meadow. Stand in the center.

She stopped looking at herself in the mirror
and started looking at herself in the moment.

As far as your appearance goes, your best side is your inside. Your radiant soul side. What part of you is making an appearance, why, and at what cost? What of your emotional appearance? Your behavioral appearance? The appearance of your heart and spirit?

The world's obsession with your appearance and the appearance of girls and women is a tide sweeping you out to the sea of soul neglect. Keep swimming back home. Don't get stranded on a lost island. If you want the peace of truth, you must obsess over your soul.

Fashion tip: Be true to yourself.
It looks good on you.

At what point did the young girl enraptured with the world, in Love with intimate kisses of discovering life, become a soul obsessed with and despairing of her appearance? The transformation happened in every moment of her life. Every comment, word, image, reaction, representation. Her whole life has been a taming of the wild in her, a redirection of her attention away from joy and into the aching abyss of self criticism.

Despair is a seducer in the night, turning you away from the light of your own soul fire. Despair in others wants the young girl in you to lose herself, then she can be used as comfort food for their despair.

We have conditioned you to desperately depend on the appearance of your backside, your chest side, your right and left side. This may have left you in disbelief over the worth and beauty of your soul side. To the point that you may not even believe it exists. It is not a myth. It is real. The truest, most affirming and glorious part of you, ripe with healing powers. If you want to bless and inspire the world, show your soul side. Its beauty has no equal.

When you learn to live in the freedom of your soul, you escape the imprisonment of surface appearance and the lifetime of crippling worry and anxiety it brings. You can recognize soul dwellers by the lightness they bring. Where they have been, peace fragrance remains. You can follow them. Or you can delight in your soul and become one. You are divinely perfect. Breathe the fragrance of this truth and be free.

Maybe your idea of your form and of the form of beauty are two separate things. This separation will always cause you to suffer. Because you are form, you are beauty. Your form and beauty are one. This is not conditional. No moments or days occur in which your form is more or less beautiful. Fluctuation is an idea in your mind. You cannot *not* be beautiful.

If you wish to feel secure about your beauty, reconcile your idea of separation. Unify your idea of your form with the truth of beauty. This may require you to release your idea of beauty, which was not your idea to begin with. Your whole life, you have been infected with a contagious idea of beauty, evolved over generations like any virus, to deteriorate how you see yourself. Beauty cannot be more or less of itself. It is immeasurable and untouchable. You cannot be more or less beautiful. Just as you cannot be more or less you. Yes, your form can change and does.

This is not your beauty changing. Only the way you see your beauty.

We can end this ancient enslavement of women. Instead of obsessing over girls' appearance, telling them they can be models, let us obsess over their souls, and tell them they can be role models. If we plant liberating seeds, we get liberating crops.

Slathering girls with beauty compliments their entire childhood creates a *call me beautiful* addiction that withers their soul and sends their identity scurrying into a tight, narrow, limited idea of who they are. Oppression and dehumanization begin when we reduce a person into a fraction of her wholeness. When she accepts, embraces, and lives inside that fraction, she has lost herself.

In a healthy life, physical beauty is jewelry around the neck of a girl's identity. It is not the entire universe of how she sees herself. Girls have the right to grow into a limitless idea of womanhood. We have a duty to behold and celebrate their wholeness, the true seeds of self Love.

Call-me-beautiful addiction is born of brain chemicals: Stimulus, reward. Over and over, since birth. To heal, Lovingly acknowledge your addiction. Go about weaning yourself. How? Love yourself in the absence of such compliments. Process such compliments for what they are: excluding of your soul. Remind yourself that people are only pointing out what they see, not what they fail to see. You can train your feel-good chemicals to flow when you think of your true, whole self, and not to flow as much when thoughts and comments are about your form. Love your formless self. Your beauty joy is endless once you discover you are forever beautiful.

True Beauty

What we see of each other's form is less than a grain of a grain of who we are. Beauty is insulted that we reduce its wondrous infinity to physical appearance. And yet beauty must agree that its appearance is beautiful, as it knows itself in all its aspects to be beautiful.

We call some of the ugliest souls beautiful. While the beauty of many souls goes unnoticed, unannounced—all because of appearance. Please do not contribute to this confusion. Don't be this kind of beauty prospector, scanning for treasures and missing all the best jewels. See into people, where soul beauty is working. See into yourself this way. Practice soul-seeing. When you see souls clearly, you are ready to live a beautiful life. Because you see it. In you. All around you. Not flares shot into a physical sky. But the lasting ethereal expression of life, also known as Love.

Make sure you are looking into the right mirror. Your soul is beautiful. Soul beauty doesn't have bad days. It just keeps shining. Soul beauty is your sole duty.

Hunting for beauty compliments leaves you starving eventually. All the compliments in the world cannot make you believe you are beautiful. You must do that work of seeing. Get down in your soil and hold your roots until they blossom in your own hands.

True beauty lives in this world the way fertility lives in a garden: subtle, simmering, sublime. It does not beg for compliments, and doesn't care if it is seen. But, oh, does it revel in the glory of its wondrous life.

If only I could show you your true beauty. You would never feel the false flame of insecurity again. You may not see your eternal beauty if you are fixated on your temporary form. How can you know you are soulfully beautiful? Do beautiful things grow around you? Beauty leaves artifacts. Love is the only true beauty, a soul duty.

If you were told since birth that your soul is beautiful, self Love would be in your precious blood. Now, tell yourself: *My soul is beautiful.* Drench your whole life in this saying. Consider the first time you told yourself you were not beautiful. Go back. Edit. Insert truth. You are beautiful in every dimension. Soak up truth, and what you express will be truthful. Here's to your radiant beauty of the soul.

Some miracles are profound beyond language. Such is you. Some beauty leaves the sky stunned and stuttering. Some brilliance has no measurement. Such is you. Some souls are a deep pot of gumbo. A wide field of clover. A continuous *Amen.* A night symphony. Conspiracy of stars. Chapel of moonlight. Chronic wonderment. Necklace of sighs. Sweet ache of labor. Persistence of pollen. Honeycomb on the tongue. Hills of wild poetry. Rivers of grace. Equatorial richness. Jubilation beneath the sea. Quivering of the dew. Such is you.

Moon Time

In your early woman seasons, during each moon you behold the release of your blood, the crimson of your soul. This intimacy with yourself, or rejection of yourself, does things to you. Grow tender and Loving with your moon flow, and your life grows soft and forgiving.

This world tries to condition you to be ashamed of your own blood, your own sacred flow, long before it first arrives. Care that you not harbor shame as you carry your life season of blood, your moon time. Your blood is as natural in you as it is natural in a man. A man's blood is a lake, never fully released or renewed. Your blood is a river. Purpose comes with this truth. Your discomfort and pain are uniquely yours. No one else can be your authority on this. Maintain your authority. It helps you manage the pain. Be your teacher, even as you seek other moon time teachers.

Your moon time is not your other times. It is your moon time. Try to make it be another time, and you suffer more. Your bleeding is worthy of honor and respect and sensitivity. From you. From others. I do not mean to dismiss your pain. I hope to help lift you into a more comforting way of holding and releasing it. You are evidence not just of birthing potential. Your moon dance also returns you over again to yourself, intensely.

When you land on this mystic planet, this moon time of yours, are you able to gain something more of yourself, or do you feel as though your life itself is weakened? I cannot know what you feel and endure. No one can fully be with you in it. Not even other women. This means you have the right and reason to celebrate your singularity of experience. Celebrate in ways that grow your Love and shed your shame. Your moon time is yours. Find your blessings in its seasons.

Bring back rites of passage. Then girls won't have to experience their first sacred flow alone, confused and scared, burrowing already into shame. Let their circle of womanhood prepare them, guide them, move them through in reassurance and celebration. A girl's sacred flow is worthy and needing of celebration. Women who still carry their own shame are afraid to celebrate in girls something too many men have made taboo. Your body coming into womanhood is never taboo. It is you. How can you be taboo?

When someone asks you if you are on your cycle, say, *I am on my purpose*. You are always on your cycle. As are men. Choose your own language to honor your body and life. A period is a punctuation point. What happens when your blood flows is not a punctuation. It is a restoration. A sacred circle. How moon song behaves.

Daughter. I Love you in your moon dress. You were made for aura. Born to glow. I see you dancing on a beach at night, wading into the warm water, your salt joining its salt. Two waters. Your blood is water, daughter. Sacred water. Don't run away. Grow familiar. Feel your potential in the pain. You don't have to sing alone. Many generations of women surround you, share this kinship, this ancestral river that runs through bodies. You deserve gentle, compassionate honor and support. Your moon time is not a weakness. It is a strength. Write songs. Join with other women and cast out shame. Shame for your womb and its ways. Shame for your body. Leave yourself awash in tender regard for your body's tenderness, rhythm, cycles, and miracle. Moonlight feels with you.

Your Hair

Your hair is a garden, a sacred growing. Let your Love and passion run wild with it. Make it your art. Never be ashamed of it. Hair shame is a poison passed around between Loved ones after it has first been poured from the chalice of those who fear you. Who yearn for your self rejection. If your hair grows toward the sky like tropical vines, or if it falls from your head as a wondrous mist, curling and waving, Love yourself in that ascension, in that falling. Your hair is the artwork of divine hands working the clay of generations. Seek out your shame and kill it. Liberate your garden, liberate yourself.

If a rebellion commences in your hair, let it be victorious. Your hair is a living thing. Like an aardvark or an avocado. It has moods and a voice. It wants to express things, yet nobody ever listens. Be that one precious listener for your hair. It carries stories and secrets, some from before your time, others that spill out in shocks and frizz, or locs and fros. And believe it or not, sometimes your hair wants rain. If you are blessed with tight coils of hair, you likely have been conditioned to be horrified by this truth. This breaks my heart. If your hair feels like doing a rain dance, to swell up into a full rain crown, who are you to oppress your hair into a timid ghost of itself. Set it free.

Sometimes your hair is inspired and wants to dance. Join it. Maybe it wants to lie down and take a nap. What a great idea. Your hair has moods. Learn to play along with your hair. It will take you unimaginable places. *Good hair* is not straight or long by definition. Good hair is *your hair*. Even the absence of your hair is good hair, as it is the absence of your own hair. Whether by choice or not, this absence is a reflection of your being; and, therefore good, as you are good. *You are goodness*. This is essential to understand. What grows from goodness is good.

Loc and curl and braid and corkscrew and plait and shave and release your hair. If they call it uncivilized, it is because they are uncivilized. They do not know your civilization. If they call it unprofessional, they are not acquainted with your kind of professional. Acquaint them. And if they call your hair unclean, their mind is filled with unclean ideas of you and your kind. Wash your own mind of their uncleanliness. Never let the lie of their stained ideas take hold in you.

Free your idea of your hair, and you free your hair. Free your hair, and you free your care. Your care for you. *Hairfulness* is a beautiful state of celebration for your artistry and life's artistry with you. When you wear itchy clothes, you scratch as long as you have them on, until your skin bleeds. You are consumed with your discomfort, not present in any moment or task. You miss meaningful things until you can get the clothes off and breathe again. This is true with your hair relations. When you are in a struggle against your hair, you wear your sadness and incarceration on your face, in your dimmed light, in your ghostly presence. When you are in a full-blown hairful revolt against what fears you, you are a light and face and heart of inspiration. Be forever careful to be wonderfully hairful, daughter of the wild.

Cosmetics

Cosmetics can be a wondrous art, or a prison of fear. The difference is not in the cosmetics. The difference is in you, daughter. A fine line exists between mascara and a massacre. No amount of makeup can hide the sadness and fear I too often see in your eyes. We believe that we can cover what we reject, that no one will see it if we bury it. But all the time, the whole world sees our burial, sees that we are a buried thing. In this way, what we seek to hide is more visible than if we had left it in peace.

If cosmetics is a true art of yours, free yourself into it joyfully. If creativity with your form springs from an authentic pulse of passion, follow that spring water as it dances out and along. Be honest with yourself about your deepest reasons for what you do and how you are. We easily convince ourselves that our self rejection is instead a form of self Love. Your soul knows the difference. It does not fall for deceitful acts. If you live in contradiction to Love, your soul suffers. If your soul suffers, all souls suffer, for all souls harbor every soul.

Hiding from yourself and the world is unfortunate. Hiding for a lifetime is tragedy. You were not born to hide. Your appearance cannot be a cause to hide. *I should hide* is a thought birthed from self rejection. *I should hide* is a nightmare thought sprung from a nightmare feeling, from a fearful rendering of *how I must look to others*. Others hardly consider your appearance. Too many are caught in a nightmare with their own appearance and life.

If you believe the more makeup you use, the more beautiful you are, you may eventually lose your face. You may literally never see it again. Your Lover and Loved ones may not see it. Your face is your featured expression. To lose your features beneath added layers means something. What does it mean to you to lose yourself? And in contrast, if you grow fearful of makeup, what does this mean for your faith in your own beauty?

She dared a new beauty product: Sacredness.

Pay close, honest attention to how you feel about your appearance. What are the roots of your feelings? Include in your daily chores time spent sifting through your thoughts, feelings, and impulses to see what comes from fear and hurt, and what comes from sacredness. Once you know what is false, you can get rid of it. What comes from sacredness, you can polish and protect.

Don't be afraid of your bare, naked face. Its divine beauty cannot be surpassed. Imagine if the sun never let this world see it without makeup. What is real will always be more glorious than what is meant to cover reality. Illusion may flutter its false wings, but it can never reach the sky. Only the truth can do that.

An artist who does not trust the canvas cannot enjoy full inspiration. Trust your natural face. Then, have fun with that, or leave it. And remember, your true, everlasting beauty needs no makeover. No improvement. Your soul is perfect. Knowing this, create cosmetically not from anxiety or fear but from pure, wild joy.

––––––

One woman listened intensely to the voice saying these words. Her eyes shone with universes dancing, spinning. She felt a burning inside. *I need to say these things*, she said to herself. As soon as she uttered this, he was saying these things. Not for her. *As her.* Her long held heaviness was coming out in a gush. Her jubilation flowed with it.

Sisterhood

I have poured many admiring tears at the beauty of your sisterhood, your resounding revival since women have been in the world. Much feeling has been shared around your circle, danced by the fire, wept, forged, resolved. I have seen you blush your power and pain into the sky together. Build, repair, defend, and rise. Sisterhood is not just a wishful notion. It is a buoyancy that keeps all of us from drowning. Humanity would not have survived without your thriving sisterhood. If you have had it in your life, you know this. If you have not been acquainted with it, I hope you go and find it.

Nurture your sisters of blood and spirit. They are your sisters in the way water is made of itself. You are made of your sisters. How can you harm them without harming yourself? Together you journey, a movement through a territory called life that too often assaults you, seeks to bury you in its dust of blindness. Fear always targets true power. Your sisters and you are true power in your *woman-ness*, which need not be defined. You know it, for you live it. In communion with others who also live it, you may find a singular power.

When we fail to nurture our singularities, those divine qualities and callings fray and decompose. If we are not careful, our singularity is lost in the storm. Sometimes we are unable to find it again. Nurture your sisters, and you strengthen the woman you are. Treat your sisters to gossip, criticism, judgment, and a hard heart, and you destroy your essence as woman. I speak of the woman you are, the woman you are destined to be. I speak of freedom.

Who benefits from your conflict with your sisters? Those who want to own you all. Those who fear your power. Those who quake at the sunrise of freedom. Some of these are women. Some are men. Others are genderless. What matters is what you build up and tear down. An old world of oppression exists for you to put to its end. As men, we must carry our own water in this. For you, try not to carry water that is not yours. Stay focused on your collective moment. Match it with your devotion.

You are not in competition. You are in communion. The world treats your sisters and you in a similar way. Rather than attack she who is already under worldly attack, use your power of compassionate empathy. You know her pain. Do not deepen it. Touch it with your understanding, for it is your pain. In this way you offer mutual medicine.

Competition over natural resources is a sad delusion. You suffer no shortage of Lovers, mates, opportunities, access. All that is for you, is already for you. No drought exists in you. This is a lie seeded in you and your sisters by wayward sisters and blinded misters. You are abundance itself. As is your sister.

Revel in each other's splendor and you discover a new altitude. A lightness of spirit. Taste this bright communion and you come to crave it. You do not have to be taught how to relate to your sisters. Another lie. Your capacity is in your marrow. You have but to awaken it. Practice. Acclimatize to its temperature. Sisterhood is a spa. Visit often. More than that, learn to live there.

If you wish for happiness and light in your life, plant it in your sisters. They will grow it and return it to you. This is a seed dispersal approach to living. Be wind-like. Treat your sisters according to what you want returned to you, and what you want to encounter as you journey.

Be kind to your sisterhood. You carry the same wounds. Climb the same mountains. Nurture the same songs. Conflict between sister-kind is a habit. A conditioning. It is not a natural state. Long have people profited from this conflict. This confusion of souls. The blood spilled is a sacredness lost.

Sister drama is a conflict diamond. Do not purchase it. Do not wear it. Do not covet it. Believe in the natural state of your sisterhood: *Peace*. So much power lives in the harmony of divine femininity that fear erupts in souls to smother that light. They believe that if you can subdue your mother, your origin womb, you become a God. Except this is not true. What is divine cannot be subdued. To try is to subdue and serrate your own soul.

Stay in the meadow of harmony with your sisters, where an abundance grows that is more than enough for everyone. Stay and know safety, inspiration, and the endless flow of your river nature. Stay and eat plenty. Grow full on the gift of what you are.

Sisterhood is tender from its wounds. When touched, it can react in pain. It can also react in power. Learn to harvest your rain. Sisterhood is a sacred basket weaving. When this weaving is tight, it holds water. All living things drink from the holding pool. Your water and your sisters' water are one ocean. Swim in that majesty, and you breathe the way wild things do.

You may be tempted to mistreat your sisters, your kindred woman souls. A sickened culture teaches you, trains you, conditions you. If you fall prey to this pattern, you are like a slave brutalizing other slaves while the master watches and laughs. As long as you abuse your sisters, you cannot heal the wounds of your own abuse. Nor can you break the chains of your oppression. Hurtfulness has never birthed wholeness. Spite remains incompatible with freedom.

Determine to keep gathering. Gatherings will keep you alive. Sometimes you share a group journey and something magical happens. You become more than friends. You become a tribe. When you gather as a tribe, all living things feel your vibration. An immense fire awakens, tilts toward your gathering. When you gather as a tribe, your power cannot be touched.

Talk story with your sisters. Story is kindling for the fire. And for your healing. Some want to keep their struggle a secret, even as they carry the struggle of others. Carrying your burdens alone does not make you a better woman. Sharing your weight lightens the way of womanhood.

Your Mother

Love your mother. Love her in her presence. Love her in her absence. Love her impermanence, for she is a fleeting thing, a continuous curling, a bright smoke dancing. You can hold her closely, though if you hold her as though she is an unchanging thing, her wellness and yours will crumble. Strive to avoid being enslaved by needfulness, by possession. She is smoke and wind.

Love her blues notes, her lifting appraisal of beautiful things. Love the way she sings. Love the Love in how she teaches you. You do not have to blindly accept or reject all she teaches you. She is neither your absolute teacher nor your adversary.

Gaze at the girl in her. How does this girl behave? Is she frenzied, feeling helpless, hopeless, unLoved? Does she bellow a beautiful song? Is your mother's inner child leading the woman, or is the woman cradling her inner child? Your mother is teaching you. How to be. Whether to be whole and alive or fragmented and run asunder. Do not idolize her blunder. Do not beat her down. Find margin with her errors. Don't drown in her hurt.

A girl's bond with her mother can be one of the most potent and enigmatic of bonds. A swirling, ardent, vining intimacy. Your Love for your mother may be strong, creating an acute magnetism. Admiration, imitation, and aversion are forces that pull your mother's spirit into you. This can include all her wonders, but also her trauma and hurtfulness. To break this trauma bind and reverse its magnetic attraction, your Love for yourself must grow to eclipse your need for your mother. Verbalize your liberation. To you. To her, even in her absence. In your creative life. Speak your new energy into life. Stalk down her hurt you have swallowed and care for it in you. Garden it from sorrow into song. You cannot heal your mother. Surrender that fixation. You can bless your mother by healing her daughter whom she Loves.

A girl must in the end sift her life from her mother's. This is the only way to freedom, and her greatest gift to both. Sift and separate her life from your life, especially as you question your life, the unequivocal path for you. Love your mother in her absence, in her neglect. Not to excuse, but to not let bitterness trespass across your peacefulness. If your mother once shared with you her milk or mood or majesty, now she could use your ministry. Your ministry of you being true to you.

And if your mother has changed to light, and walks with the ancestors, find her there. Sing yourself to her through your Love notes. When you arrive to her diaphanous striding, aside a sea of souls, Love her there. Love her changes, her tenure, her temperament. Love this new song she sings, this purified melody freed from the world yet more in the world. She is with you now as spirit, as the breath of Creation drafting your warm air. As a bird, a thing with wings.

Love your mother. Not for her. For you. You are filling your tank, your capacity for being a living thing. That you may pour out more stew to the hungry, more tears for the thirsty, more salt. More soul. More surrender.

You don't have to inherit your parents' pain. Or pass it on. If you have been scalded, anger will not treat your wounds. Do not imitate the ways that harmed you. Plant new seeds. Be the one to end the cycle. Love yourself profoundly. Sink into a hot bath of compassion, over and over, until your terror peels away. Love yourself to life.

Be patient with your mother. She listens to you in her language, even if it is not her language. Even as she tries to learn yours. If you need distance, Love yourself enough to let sky grow between the two of you and soothe the way.

Your desire to please your mothers and fathers can be the death of your life, your light, your calling in the world. It can also be a healthful breath in your freedom sky. Becoming you takes a lifetime. How wonderful is that? You have been given your whole life, whatever its length, to craft your fullness. Becoming you is no more than being you. As you are revealed to you, your sense of being you changes. This is not evidence of your failure. It is the wonder of the journey. In the end, being you honors your countless mothers.

Motherhood

You in motherhood is sacred. You not in motherhood is also sacredness. In it or out of it does not matter as much as how are you in it or out of it. Do you mourn? What do you do with your mourning? How you carry your grace matters. Gestation is a part of mothering. As are birthing, nurturing, and letting go. Among these, do you have weak muscles? You can always grow stronger.

Societies are good at celebrating motherhood. Often poor at honoring and caring for mothers. How is your honoring of yourself, or other mothers? Have you sat with your ways of honoring, shared tea with them, and grown more acquainted? It helps to know your ways.

How you honor women who are *not mothers* means as much as how you are with mothers. Both life rivers feed the greater river of motherhood. All women are mothers.

When you use another person to fulfill your desire for children, you violate all three of your lives, and more. A child born of self serving action inherits suffering, as does the family and beyond. When you honor another person's sovereign life by moving honestly into having children together, each soul is enriched. Reasons for having children vary. The relational road we take to arrive matters. It becomes the spirit of a child's life.

The idea that you must be a perfect mother may kill the peace and spirit of both you and your child. The idea that a mother is a supreme being, greater than a father, greater than a childless woman, greater than all, is a death molecule. Supremacy is poison. Keep your immune system of identity strong enough to resist this idea. Carrying this expectation of perfection cripples the chance for peace in your child, in you, and between you. It creates a massive impulse for control, for smothering, for not allowing yourself or your child to breathe.

All your relationships suffer inside this perfection delusion and your upkeep of it. No one is allowed to be herself. No one is valued fully. Everyone is chained to serving this idea of your perfection. How sad, for in motherhood, you are given an immeasurable gift of wonderful imperfection.

You inherit a crushing imposition, the expectation that you must have children. This steals from you the freedom of enjoying a sheer, pure desire for children. And the freedom of not desiring children. You do not deserve to spend your life judging yourself and being judged. If you live life racing a mothering clock, all your relationships suffer. Especially your experience with you.

How intimately acquainted are you with the reasons you want or don't want to have children? Not the reasons you tell yourself. The truth beneath, that you may not wish to touch? Your reasons, if you do have children, will touch your children's entire lives, and your generations without end. Be willing to touch your reasons.

Maybe you burn with a desire to have children. Do you burn with the same desire to have yourself? If you have children but don't have yourself, your having children can bring an even deeper emptiness, a never-abating guilt that even with the gift of children you are still not happy. This is harmful to your children and to you. *I want to have children one day.* This has been repeated countlessly. Some of the most joyful souls learn to repeat a precious kind of birthing mantra: *I want to have myself someday. Lots and lots of myself.*

The words *having children* can create suffering. We do not *have* children. We let them through. They are a glory we witness, with an assignment we have not written.

Being a *good mother* is a vague notion. A trap of propaganda rarely examined. Being a safe mother is a more concrete reality. We can assess safety by examining whether children feel safe with their mother. And whether a mother feels safe with herself. Safe from all forms of harm. Safe from verbal and emotional violence and coping dysfunction. Safe to communicate openly and truthfully. If you wish to be a safe mother, look to mothers whose children feel safe with them.

The way sun kisses earth. That. Is a mother.

As a mother, you are not raising children. You are raising your own wellness and unwellness inside your children. They are being raised by life, with your life a vital contributor. They are deltas. You are a river pouring your sediment and life into their blooming waters. Sons and daughters. Not your limbs. Your encounter to behold.

As a woman without children, you are not a childless woman. You are filled with all the children who still need you. You see them every day. Your heart clenches, melts, aches, wonders. See how your life pours into them even without formal titles of belonging? They long for your longing. You have every right and calling to be with them, not only physically, but in the way you live your life.

I see the glory of your journey. Motherhood is a continuous letting go. Of your child's many seasons. Your journey is also a persistence of faith. How to Love something delicate and vulnerable in this world and still believe harm will not befall that precious soul?

Our Love for our children must be greater than our fear of acting on their behalf. Our Love must be the greater fire. For you who sacrifice dearly on the altar of your Love, life bows down to you in generations. We see you. Goodness is your legacy. Glory is your holy name.

Humanhood

Humanhood is not a thing we are born with. Nor is it a title. Humanhood is a way of being. It allows us to move beyond survival into the realm of being alive. Not all are born human. Only those who savor Love and compassion achieve this high regard. Some take a lifetime to arrive. Some never do. Some arrive again and again in every moment, for their joy of renewal is irresistible, and their souls abide in grace.

Humanity will not fulfill its promise until womanhood is held sacredly. Until girls and women no longer fear for their lives, nor spend life reclaiming their wholeness, gathering scattered dignities like shattered sea shells. Until they have no reason but to assume the flowering of their dreams. It should not ever occur to a girl that she is in jeopardy by birth, nor should she ever begin the sad burrowing into self betrayal. Words like *civilized, advanced, modern, developed*, and *enlightened* are a ferocious sham. We are not yet the nobility of our fable. And yet, a tide rises that will sweep sacredness into the sky. That will be our new sun. And humanity will breathe an entire breath for the very first time.

Elderhood

We have trained you to devalue your elders. They are not poor or pitiable. They are a wealth we have taught you to scorn. You impoverish yourself by cutting them out from your breast and discarding them. They are the source of your sap, the milk of your marrow. You cannot thrive without your elder tree. You are seeking something, so you may be depressed, anxious, and lonely. What you seek, they have gathered abundantly. And if you seek it from them, they will grow more alive, for sharing with you activates life in them.

They fade when you are not living, and because you are not alive in their elder living. Can you see this circle? It cannot afford to be broken. If you see your elders, open your heart. Bow down. Gather stories. Honor their journey that has endured since long before you. Honor what you do not know, what you cannot see, what you are yet unable to feel. Honor your future now alive in them. This is how you feed your future. You are on your way to becoming an elder.

Treat your aging as your precious art. Not for gallery display. For your pleasure and garden of meaning. For sharing with others through vitality. If you run from aging, it will catch you. It is faster and has endless endurance. If you take a deep breath and walk with aging, singing to it, it will become a faithful companion. It will be addicted to your walks together. It will also entertain you along the way, like a puppy. You will cry, marvel, and laugh. Be close with your aging. The relationship will bless you. Look into the mirror, and as ritual, say, *Thank God I am aging. And this is my holy art.*

Go to the redwoods and move through their society. Touch their skin. Feel the old drumming inside their breast. Gaze at their enormity and feel their stillness. Then you cannot tell yourself at any age that you are not young and strong, not creative and vital. You cannot say you do not have offerings for your people and a voice that quiets the wind. You cannot claim to be without the power of shade and sunlight, repose and seedfulness. That you are not at the center of the circle of life and your people, that they do not depend on you and your stories, and presence, and seeing. Go to the redwoods and be acquainted with the finery of your age and tenure.

Others call it aging.
You shall call it refining your art.
Re. Fine. Yourself.

If you tell yourself, *I am old*, you will become old. You will succeed at making your judgment true. You will speak yourself into decrepitude. If you tell yourself, *I am full of life*, you will overflow with life. Your words have more than power. They have your truth in them. They are prophecy. As you live, you gain life. You don't lose it. Taste that vintage? You are becoming a better wine.

You may feel you have been living a long time. That you are old. If you are alive, you are in your prime. If you are alive, you are young. New things are happening in each moment. Your cells, tissue, and the world beyond you are a divine turning, a flush fountain of phenomena. Discoveries abound, more than you can enjoy at once. Refine this masterpiece of being you, taste life anew.

As you live, your hair may change to white or silver. See this as a symbol. Maybe when you were younger, your hair color absorbed sunlight. Once changed, it reflects sunlight. This is not about hair color. It is about your role in the human community. Younger, you needed much nurturing. Now, you are needed as a nurturer. As a giver of light. Do you feel shame about your years? This is likely because the culture has shamed you. Shame on us. People are lost from themselves, and in the process have lost recognition of the sacredness of generations, of the honor due to their elders. If you spend Loving time with your shame, you can diminish it. Then you can move shamelessly through the world, giving off light.

Do not grieve your outer beauty. It has increased.
Learn to see it with universal eyes.

Love the white snow and silver streams of your hair. Love it because of what it holds: Life. Stories. Meaning. Your face and its lines are treasure chests. Your aches and even the way you may perceive time to quicken are all the gathering of meaning. Life is meaning if it is anything. In this way, you are more alive in your elder years. More full of wonderful oceans of meaning.

If you water the seeds in you that say, *I should slow down now. I should deteriorate now. I should die now,* those thoughts will be fulfilled. In a land far from here, I once came across a man several hundred years old. He whispered something to himself as he walked the ridge above a rice paddy. Morning's sun crossed his shoulders, a bright robe. I asked him what he was whispering. He said he was whispering his mantra: *I am alive.*

We tend to forget we are alive. As you become richer in years, it is good to remind yourself, *I am alive*. Especially if culture is always telling you it is time for you to fade away. Or that you shouldn't be living as much anymore. Bring these untruths and any shame in you to the fire of your Loving attention. Examine them in the firelight. Then, when you understand them for what they are, throw them in the fire. Let them burn.

Your Seasonal Life

You are a seasonal creature. At any time of year, when you feel spring inside, bloom. When you feel summer, shine. If fall murmurs, slow, turn, shed. At winter's mood, take your repose. Rest in quietude. Be in close touch with your seasons. They can change by the moment and day. They are your teachers, your caregivers. Be attentive. Your life will ease and flourish. Resist your seasons, and suffer. Live in your seasons. You will know peace.

Behold nature for its predictable lessons. Learn when to let go. Learn when to embrace. Sky does not interrupt the rainbow, or rush it, or resist its passing. This is why sky knows peace. Change can be an illusionist, making you believe it is a mountain, when really it is only a sand grain dissolving in the winds of gracious time. When you feel fear over a change in your life, breathe. Remember that what you perceive is only a grain of sand.

In the end, she discovered
it was only the beginning.

Patience is not just a hoped-for quality to laugh at and not grow into. Patience is the nature of peace. You cannot have peace without patience. Patience is an unconditional spirit. If you have it for some things and not others, you do not have patience.

Aging and youthfulness each have a purpose. You are gifted with a chance to discover this meaning. Believe it is there, and you will explore joyfully, cherishing each moment along the way. That you are forever changing is a miracle of shedding and birthing. Witness the glory inside your universe.

Receive these words at age 18 and 28 and they will be two different languages. At 68 they will be from a different species. Words don't hold the truth. We do, as we peer deeply into them and see ourselves. I cast out to you this language as seeds. If you are ready to be born, you will swallow and cradle them for the journey. If you want to stay in your womb of comfort, eventually the muffled sounds outside will frustrate you and you will come forth into the music.

Leaves and branches speak to you of the seasons of your life. Something in their relationship says, *It's okay to let go*. Letting go is what made you. You have been part of a great turning all along. Something is next, a cause for wonder. Let the wind decide.

Be in Love with the seasons of your life. Love your way through. You are not being moved from moment to moment. You are moving your moments. You are the thing that is happening to each moment. See your proactive role, and you lose anxiety that comes from feeling helplessly swept along. Moments. Meaning. Memories. To collect them with all your heart is to live. Seed. Sprout. Shoot. Stalk. Flower. Fruit. Feel each season of your life. Cherish your endless births.

Manhood

The idea of *woman* and *man* has created great suffering in woman and man. From birth and prior, the hammering is forceful and unceasing. No child can escape the undertow sweeping them away from divine truth. We abandon our uniqueness in a desperate scramble to be accepted by the herd, to remain at its center and not its periphery, where the air can be a discouraging cold. This gravity of the center creates immense delusions.

People live their lives in these cages, wondering why they hurt badly, why such distance looms between woman and woman, woman and man, man and man. Daughter, you have a way out. Follow your spirit deep into your womanhood. Sever the bindings of expectation. In time, you will arrive to your unique womanhood and clearly see, for the first time, the essence of manhood.

Don't ask yourself what a man would do.
Ask what a woman would do
who is free as a man.

You have no need to compare yourself to maleness. No one knows what a male is. Or what a female is. Knowing is not our human realm. Believing you know is an atmosphere that breeds prejudice. Let yourself not conspire to enlist in ideas about maleness and femaleness. Compare yourself to what your soul says, to what your spirit discerns, to what your heart bleats. Compare not to myths. Doing that is self betrayal ending in lonesome wandering and unnecessary harm. Practice not comparing. Gift your life in this way.

You don't have to be the opposite of male, more than male, more or less male-like. You don't have to be a man, conquer men, or accommodate men. These are slaveries. You can be a woman in whatever way you wish. And you can go beyond that. In a soulful sense, you are a shape shifter. You can be anything you want to be. You are all things. Whole and complete. Kill the seed of insufficiency humans have buried in you. You are abundance. You are all four seasons, the four elements. Every prophet's sermon lives in your marrow. Don't live as a flightless arrow. Sing through the air on fire with your soul song.

You may assume a man knows what it means to be a man. He may have been taught by others who do not themselves know manhood. You may assume a woman knows what it means to be a woman. She may have been taught by others who themselves were misled. Appraise your teachers carefully. If you choose your teachers by status, wealth, social power, or even their kinship to you, they may lead you away from your truth and not into it.

Even if every man you have known has treated you the same way, still you are not close to knowing all the ways of man. Be responsible for the ideas about men that you pass on to other women. They will be blessed or harmed by those ideas, for they are only ideas. Empower them to discover the truth in their own hopeful way.

The deepest place in a true man is not sexual desire. It is soul desire. If you have known a true man, you know this. Men need and yearn for the same soulfulness women do. Do not let our many expressions of soul desire confuse or mislead you.

Many boys are never taught that their natural lust is not the same thing as romance. That lust isn't an access key, but a personal desire requiring reciprocation. That lust is meant to be carried forth in the honoring river of relationship. That lust is to be managed within oneself, not imposed on others recklessly. This is what it means to be a man. Or an adult. Your body is not a permission slip for the lust of others. It is a sacred monument. Preserve your land.

If you are approached lustfully, this can be your opportunity to teach how you expect to be treated. If a person is not interested in your teaching, then maybe that person does not qualify to be in your class.

You have the right to make eye contact and not have it be taken as an invitation. Experience may have left you hesitant to look at people, especially yourself. Go ahead. It's safe. Make eye contact with your soul.

Do you believe that if you serve a man's ego and desires, you will keep him? Keep him as a friend, colleague, father, brother, or Lover? Your strategic servitude cannot keep a man. Men, like all souls, are with you in either Love or fear. Without his Love or fear, your servitude holds little power. Know that you have your Love to offer. Believe in it. Have faith in its fertility and resonance. Your Love is an earth bed. In that ground, men, as with all people, can grow the roots of their Love, strengthening them to dissolve the roots of their fear. Let go of the idea of keeping. You will lose. Embrace your power to grant freedom. You will gain much more than that.

Some men appear to resent women. Look beneath the surface storm. Down deeper you find that they fear the intensity of their soul attraction. People are drawn to and fear the origin of things. We fear our vulnerability, tenderness, strength, birth pain. Some men also fear not knowing. Women are a painful mystery to some men. If they cannot feel competent, they cannot feel control. This triggers tender insecurity: usefulness, worth, value. A man who appears to despise women is likely to despise himself, particularly for his secret need for women.

Do not underestimate the presence in the world of men who deeply honor women. They are not mythical creatures. They exist in every community, their hearts breaking at the dishonor and pain. In the grain of their living, they are teaching and correcting boys, girls, men, and women about honor. If you ask why a man would care deeply about the safety and freedom of girls and women, you must not know what it means to truly be a man.

Too many girls become women who shrink to accommodate men. Too many boys become men who swell to eclipse women. Both women and men teach these ways to our children. We have vast undoing to do.

The male gaze does not have to be your tyrant. When you feel it, gaze your soul. This will make you strong. The male gaze may feel powerful, but it is no more than the mist of perception. A gaze is a gaze. Your soul is everything.

When you crack open the hard shell that is many men, you find the soft soul of a boy saying, *All I ever wanted was to feel, to be a river. I never asked to be a shell.*

Young boys acting harmfully are trying to return to the safety of the womb. Recognize their fear. Take care not to empower it, but to empower them to recognize it. Their fear is their journey. It is not on you to travel it for them. To do that is to give up your journey and freedom.

You have the power to raise your sons to be the kind of men you wish to encounter in the world. I refer now to every son. For every son is your son. Each time you Lovingly touch a son, you raise the sun. Your tone of voice brings *sonrise*. Your discipline, your story, your dignity all lift up the son. And how you raise a daughter becomes the way she raises her son.

Boys struggle mightily to comprehend the meaning of their bodily strength. The world teaches them false lessons. Physical force isn't the greatest force. Let us raise boys into a harmony with the world, an honoring manner, a bravado for doing no harm. Even the strongest man can be the gentlest man. Muscles and sensitivity are not opposites. They make up true men.

We call men gentlemen, even as we celebrate their physical *ungentleness*. We are confused, thus our boys are confused. You have the power to raise, nurture, and teach strong, gentle men. Let us stop bruising the world by misleading our boys. It is time for a new lesson and language. From here forward, as humans, let us in every way say to our sons, *Just because your force can destroy and dominate doesn't mean you have the right. Restraint and gentleness make a boy a man.*

Physical Presence

Sometimes you feel like a sand grain bounced between boulders in a world teeming with the bodies of men. Some men are with their bodies as babies with new winter clothes—clumsy with the bulk, uncoordinated. Others use their bodies as masks against their fear. Our insensitivity with our male size and force can leave you bruised, feeling unsafe, eclipsed, fearful, angry. In those moments, remember the size and power of your soul body. You are not small or weak. You never were. You were born into a world where everyone misunderstands who they really are, lost in their form, lost from their light.

Your soul size suits you.
Your measurement is infinity.
Keep expanding.

Grant yourself permission to live in your soul light. To permeate spaces. Not to dominate. To exist fully. Remember, the boy in every man is still himself fearful and insecure. While the man in every boy still longs to let himself feel vulnerable again. In our often careless, reckless physical movement and positioning, we men do not feel as mountainous as it may seem. And you, in your womanhood, are a magnificent mountain.

If you are deeply rooted in the divine size of your spirit and soul, this can help you overcome feelings of being overpowered, unsafe, or vulnerable. *Smallness* is an acute psychology that holds us down, pulls us into fear. You are not in this world because you are small. You are not small. You are endless phenomenon. Ants and aphids know nothing of their smallness. They live full, creative lives. You may say, *But they can be crushed easily.* As can a mountain in an earthquake. While microscopic bacteria can break down the most gigantic of things. Physical size and strength need not determine you. You are already determined. Endowed of soul. You can live a size life. Or you can live a soul life. Mantra your right to this every day.

Gender

Enter the genderless realm of Love. Liberation alleviates suffering. Love is a truth and an atmosphere. In that atmosphere, gender does not exist. This is not to say woman and man do not exist within Love. Woman and man exist freely in Love's dimension. Not in the way we perceive ourselves on earth. But in the way we roam as spirit manifest in body, imbued with the mystic purpose of our bodies—structures and dynamics for fruitful lives.

They say you are some kind of witch in the woods. I say you are the weeping of the moss. Laughter of the fox. You are the light in the clearing and the birthing shade beneath the canopy. My words are a prayer song and I am praying. That you will not invite inside your soul the myths told of women and men. This is how you lose yourself and the possibility of finding the nectar of others.

I pray you remember from your time before birth that a truth exists far beyond these tiny polarities, these insecure conflicts positing woman and man. Whatever they tell you is a woman, bring it to your soul fire and cook it. If it fills the air with a scent that romances your spirit, eat it. If it lifts into a strange smoke that stings, cast it away from you.

Whatever they tell you is a man, do the same with that. These myths have buried mountains of human promise. Poisoned endless streams. Set fire to these ideas they bring you like a nervous rain. Set fire and observe how the burning feels. Stay close to your fire.

Discern not to swallow poisonous things you come across in the marshes and meadows. When you find yourself in places of apparent beauty, what might kill you lurks in the busy grass. See instead the open field that is woman or man. Look not for the fence line. Look up and see what is looking down at this splendor. If you set out at sunrise seeking the boundary of woman or man, by sunset you will have gathered a thousand evidences of nothing and your stomach will burn with emptiness. Let go of the burning rope of boundary and you will find women and men. And you will see them for all of what they are.

Your Father

Cherish and celebrate the Loving presence of your father. Do not assume that because he is your father, he must Love or care for you in a certain way. His way is his way. Record the ways of his gentleness. Of his firmness. He can be hard clay or soft sand. Pay attention to how he Loves. Learn from that. Take away lessons, weave baskets to hold your own water, your own Love ways. Watch closely how he feels. How he heals. How he remembers and forgets. What is he doing with the boy inside his soul? How does he chase after or sit with his father?

Your father is living a fatherhood with you, a thing that is often devalued as less than motherhood. Has this bruised him? Does he doubt himself, beat himself up? Or is he determined to be a full parent even as others assume him to be a fraction of a parent? Gather meaning from all of this. Your father is a window into your relationship with life. How you treat your father is a practice ground for how you treat all living things.

Speak to your father. Your voice can awaken him to his own truth and healing. He needs to know how you feel about him. How you feel about how he feels about himself. Show him in your native language how he treats himself. Be a mirror. Take care not to be his crutch or cradle. Do not cripple your life. Your father has his own path to travel. His water is his own weight. You do not owe your father. Your obligation is to Love. Love, in turn, offers itself to your father in his every breath. The owing is his. He owes himself that he Love himself.

No other man can ever be your father. No matter how wonderful another man is, he is his own soul. To expect him to replicate your father, or fill up the spaces left behind by any neglect of your father is to expect him to perform an unachievable magic. To the extent that you expect or seek this in another man, you dishonor who he actually is. You dishonor the relationship you could have. You dishonor yourself.

Grieve the absence of your father, no matter the manner of his absence. Do your healing duty in the place of your wound. This wound can easily mix with other wounds, creating a wound confusion. This may cause you to direct your feelings in wild directions, spraying anger, hurt, and hope into spaces where they do not belong. This is how we end up as prey. Predators have an eye for what scrambles around on the ground looking for shelter.

Love your father in the ways he is available in form or spirit. This takes great courage if you have a deep well of anger or resentment to penetrate. Love the boy you imagine him to have been, the person before his own wounding, before he learned false lessons. Love the soul he was sent here as, the life he was meant to be. Love his potential as a soul beyond his role in your life. Love him as the father he dreamed of being. The one he kills himself for not being. Love your father. Love him in his enduring fear, for his imperfect running away from life.

Love your father. Not for him. For you. That you may heal, daughter. Love his natural scent, his native heartbeat, his sensitivity, however it is wired or has been rewired. Love his voice and language, dreams and hopes. Love his pain. Love it deeply. Knead into it with your sturdiness, the strength you can gather. Sink your fingers deep into his despair and knead the bread of his soul. You will always need him, in the way we need what we come from. This need not be a binding, a sourness. It can be yeast in the rising of what you knead in him. In you. In everything.

Break the unwellness that may course through your generations. Love your father in the way you let go of a petal or a cotton seed—lightly, tenderly, bravely leasing it to the wind to care for, blessing yourself in tears of surrender. Say, *I do not own this man, this soul. No matter what he should have been, how he should be, what I want so badly it breaks even the breaking of me. I do not own this man. I set him free. I Love my father.*

Feel all of your ancestral fathers. They have been with you always. Their gaze and Love will be with you ever. It is not enough that you think of them. Feel them. You are not fatherless. You are being fathered with a complete Love possible when body life becomes soul life entire.

Do not lose yourself in the land of absence, spending life suffering through thoughts and feelings about the way he wasn't present for you. Instead, find yourself in the land of presence. In what ways is he present in you? Think of him not as an individual, but as an entire ancestry. You are a reflection of a lineage of generations, not individual imperfections and failings. What awesome legacy, and source of your soul beauty and aspiration. Parents are a canvas on which you paint the mural of self knowledge.

The contrast that gives you definition. An explanation from which you clarify yourself. An altitude from which you gain your chosen altitude.

Fatherhood

I celebrate the way you honor fatherhood even as you suffer the failings of some fathers. If you do not, children taste your bitterness. It seeps into their bones and becomes their self hatred and broken harmony with fatherhood. This entire world is the fruit and tenderness and hurt and hope of fatherhood. You cannot separate yourself from it. Not by anger or spite. Not by control or denial. Your only peace and hope lie in cherishing true fatherhood, which is a success, not a failing. A presence, not an absence. An endurance, not a retreat.

For a child, no such thing exists
as a meaningless father.

A true father does not force a child into a father-child relationship. He lets that relation grow from Love. A father is not a force of possession. He does not care for common ideas about fathers. His life and fatherhood are not tied to expectation. They spring from his soul. Eternal affection and devotion guide a true father. Even if society does not see him or believe in him. He is a fountain of faith. In himself, his child, and their relationship. And in his child's sovereign journey beyond his life.

You, daughter, have an opportunity to bless the world. Support and honor and celebrate any true fathering you encounter. Put your whole heart into it. So it grows.

Your Inner Life

Learning to have an inner life is like getting used to being outside in nature at night. At first, you can't see anything and fear takes over. But if you stay with it, you start seeing everything clearly and a peace grows in you that sets you free. Do not fear yourself. Spend the time.

Inner peace, freedom, and beauty require that you keep your spirit clean. Harmful seeds are always being dropped into your garden. Many stories you live inside are neither true nor native to your soul. Tending your roots and removing pestilence are worth the effort. Abundance and clarity are your reward.

Your soul is a perfect fire. If you want warmth and companionship, stay close to it. Often we wander away from the one thing we need most. Tonight, get cozy with your inner aura. It knows how to be tender with you. In the morning, don't leave your soul behind. Watch sunrise together. Go out into the world an inseparable tandem. Peace, that mystic medicine, will flood your being. And you will be whole. You will taste true bliss.

Wanting to remember who she truly was,
she held ceremony with her soul.

Socialize with your soul. The soul itself does not grow lonely. But you do, without your soul time. In your private gardening, poverty and wealth of the soul begin. Your own soul should be the last place foreign to you.

We spend much of our lives seeking outward relief for our persistent suffering and fears. Grasping externally for happiness. All along the answer is inward, where our Love grows. Balance matters. It is not that we ought to avoid an outer life, but that we need not neglect our innerness. It is possible to lose yourself in the world, to be dissolved into that ocean. We also have the power to return home.

Sometimes home seems far away. It's a short trip. Just one turn.

She made only one turn and she was home.
She turned inward.

It hurts to be a runaway. You are cold, scared, hungry, and feel more alone than ever. You imagine others in the warmth of their homes and beds, surrounded by Loved ones, and full of peace. You look into windows craving what you see others having. This is the story of your life when you run away from your soul. Fortunately, you can always come home. Your perfect meal, bed, warmth, and companionship await.

Are you tired, daughter? Fatigued down to the bone? Maybe your power has been disconnected for too long. Connect your life to your soul, and your soul to its source. Spending time with your own soul heals everything. Even the world.

Early in life, it is easy to fall in Love with the world. Overcome with outward wonder and awe, you gradually abandon your innerness. Your tide of suffering increases before you are aware. Your precious sands of peace have been swallowed. You want someone, somewhere. You are that person. You are that place. Come home.

Your soul is a perfect, custom-made home. Live in it. If you want to feel something wonderful, feel your own soul. Orchestrate a full moon in your soul sky. Let Love light the lantern. Want your own soul more than anything. It is the only thing to which you have guaranteed access. Your soul is the most beautiful place you will ever visit. Go as often as you can.

She stopped worrying about finding herself
and fell in Love with what she found.

Your inner sky is a climate you determine. You get to choose your own weather. What a wondrous gift. If you allow it to happen, your soul can be your sky, your sunlight, your sanctuary, your song, your story, your life.

Your soul is its own prophet. Listen to it and you will know the music of your own truth moving like fresh spring water through the glory and mystery of life.

The most arduous, rugged social change begins and endures with the gentle, brave breaking apart and putting back together of personal identity. Soul work is a private root of the public flower of social change.

Your truest Love often feels painfully far away. When this happens, open your heart and pour out glory to the world. This will be your Love letter. To your true Love. Which is your soul.

If you feel lonely, it may be because you have not gone home to yourself in a long, long time. You are waiting for *you*. Maybe you are spending your life looking for a way out. The only way out is in. At last, journey and befriend your soul. It is *you* who your soul wants most.

What are the endangered species in the territory of your soul? Love, kindness, compassion? Joy, hope, laughter? Patience, faith, virtue? Honesty, nakedness, truth? Be kind to yourself. Survey your wild animals. Spend time with those populations dwindling inside you. Practice this conservation and you can repopulate the world.

You have an outside voice and an inside voice. Your outside voice is the voice of others outside of you. Your inside voice is the voice of your soul. As often as possible in this blizzard of voices, use your inside voice.

Look at us. All of us. We are infinity, wishing we had more power. We are eternity, wishing we had more time. Not knowing yourself creates a terrible anxiety. Not being true to the self you know creates an even worse anxiety.

You travel the world seeking wonders. The greatest wonder is your soul. It is pristine. It cannot be desecrated by tourists. You cannot be overcharged for the visit. Bad weather doesn't affect the experience. No airports. No stress. Book a trip. The travel is easy. Close your eyes. Breathe deeply. You have arrived.

You are trained to see only your body. Your heart and soul become myths you fail to water. They wilt from your neglect. Each day, see your entire being. Don't get lost in the mirror staring at your face and form. Gaze at your spirit and its dreams. Behold your essence, your ancestors dancing wildly, your prayers spread like a golden meadow, the answers flocking thick and glorified. See yourself. This is how you begin to nurture yourself. What you see you touch, water, feed, sing to.

See yourself, to avoid catching the fever of needing to always be seen. The seeing others do of you is too often superficial. They spy your surface water and feed you compliments void of nutrition. Your deep water drowns, starves, wails. You respond by scavenging for more compliments. This needfulness is a killing cycle. A dead zone. You are meant to live as more than a hungry ghost. Host blazing rebellions against ideas that reduce you. Don't be seduced. You are sky, sun, song, subtle seeping synonyms for sacredness. Be these things, completely.

Meet reduction with enlargement. Respond to erasure with bold fonts of you. Graffiti your life in your native colors. You are not a condition to be cured. You are the cure for soulless conditions. Retain your self Loving composure. Treasure your peculiar persona, your quirky qualities. These are powers blessed into you, as divine design is blessed into each snowflake. Without you being you, you are impoverished with an absence no one can fill. Clenching, grabbing, grasping, attaching—these are spasms of fear. Practice them and you court suffering. All things smother and die when held too tightly. Practice peace as you let life's butterflies land on you, be with you, and lift away from you.

Practice not owning. Owning is an illusion. It locks you in nervousness, in fear of losing what you can never lose because you can never possess it to begin with. What tragedy if you live your entire life as if to say, *Look at me! Want me! Love me!* You are a created thing. You have always and will always be looked at, wanted, and Loved, perfectly. You are the evidence you seek. Your existence is proof. What you do and do not do, does not change this.

What if your soul could open far more than you know? What if it is a vast womb of galaxies, of visions eternal and divine? Maybe your soul is sky with no boundary, or an aching flower dying to be born to blossom. It could be night, host of stars, or dawn spreading its ocean of light. Your soul could be that bright. It could be the miracle you have sought your whole life, the question and answer entwined and wildly mating. Fire. Your soul could be fire. You could be its air. If you open.

Solar power is nothing compared to soul power. Solar power can energize civilization. Soul power can energize endless generations and heal us back to being human. If you want to invest in the most promising renewable energy, pour yourself into a life of the soul.

So many seek holiness in the world, but few seek the holiness inside their souls. The world is a lookout point to behold the world of spirit with mortal eyes. Look in. What you see will be your window to look out. *Look out*, you don't want to miss this amazing grace.

Don't prospect for gold in an apple tree. Don't scour a cornfield for treasure buried in beach sand. Get your coordinates right. Peace is in your bones. Joy. Hope. Soul satisfaction. All lie within, inside this miracle of now, this paradise that is your inner life.

Inner Stillness

Stillness can be counterintuitive to the modern mind. Which is why the modern mind goes insane. Sanity, in a spiritual sense, is not the capacity to process information in a frenzy of anxious multitasking. It is a state of being that brings you in harmony with the rhythm and sacred weaving of nature. Stillness is a consequence of being at peace with the Great Mystery that is life. A comfort with being near yourself. Modern life is a poverty of rushing and distraction. Gift yourself. Stay home in your soul.

Stillness is the behavior of forests. Of deer by a stream. A canyon misted in sunrise. Even a brook can be still as it runs. For it runs with a knowing of what it is, and is content with that. Butterflies don't land on anxious flowers grasping for their beauty. They land on flowers fulfilled with their own beauty and not grasping. This is how peace chooses where to go.

Be still. Peace is a butterfly looking
for a safe place to land.

Slow down. Practice not doing. Peace doesn't grow in the vortex of your anxiousness. It grows in the meadow of your stillness. After all, it is a flower. Let your thoughts go, and they will sing. You will know peace. Love yourself with rest. You are under no obligation to keep your mind busy. Let go of your kite string. Your deepest healing happens when you release your lifelong habit of worrying, and let all that you are relax into peace. Even a moment of nothingness is a gift that leaves you new.

Your thoughts will be okay without you. Rest.

Meditation is sabbatical for the soul. But you don't have to call it meditation or mindfulness or Zen. When you name it, it dies inside your attachment to the name. You squeeze the life out of it. Instead, just choose it. Choose to shift your attention back to your center, your breath, your being. Keep choosing, for a second, a minute, an hour. When you drift, keep choosing to come back. One day, your choosing will become a habit with no name.

Wild meditation is free of intellectual ribbons, rules, and ideologies. It is not defined by where you meditate, how, with whom, or for how long. It is free. It is you breathing yourself back to you. You untucking your soul from its tight social bed, letting it be a jubilant hawk drafting, a laughing monk, naked and wildly running into the miracle we call a moment. If you can keep your meditation wild, free from culture club expectations, it can be one of your greatest revelations.

Inner stillness and silence act like fishing nets, allowing you to catch epiphanies like schools of fish. Slow down, grow quiet, and catch your quota. Birds flock to trees of inner stillness, no matter how much their branches move. Peace flocks to souls with inner stillness, no matter the outer turbulence stirring.

An apple on a tree does more in stillness than you can ever do in busyness. You, too, can make sugar in your soul. Be still. Let Peace gather in you. If you grow still inside and listen, you will hear all the beautiful whispers of your soul. The way a mountain sits and ponders is inspiration for a peaceful life.

Life is always whispering, *Be still. Move.* Peace is being in both states at once. In deep stillness lives the sweetest movement. In true movement the soul grows wonderfully still. Chase wind across the desert. This balance is dance, the pauses and poses expressing as much as the motion. This is life.

It is easy to sit outside and let the breeze wash over you. You don't try to grab, hold, possess, judge, or control the breeze. You don't mistake the breeze for being you. You just sit peacefully in the breeze. Do the same with your thoughts. Sit peacefully and let them wash through you. Let them go on their way. They are not you. They are weather passing through. Sit peacefully in your breeze.

Expecting the mind not to think is like expecting sky to have no weather. Weather is the nature of the atmosphere. Thinking is the nature of the mind. Think beautifully. Let your thoughts float through you and away. Inside your brain, heart, and soul you are painting a powerful mural with every thought. Make it beautiful.

Like water, peace flows into open spaces. Be emptiness. When you finally grow still inside, your soul opens. Becomes sky. Now, at last, peace has room to roam. Like soft, silent snowfall, may peace come unto you.

Inner Peace

Daughter, press your face against this sky of blue, this sea of sun. Know what peace feels like when it touches a living thing. Peace is the fragrance you seek, the perfume of your very nature. You cannot avoid your own soul. You must reckon with it. Stop fleeing and start being. Only then arises peace. For the source of peace is not in the world. It is in your soul.

*Your next breath. That's how long
you have to wait for peace.*

Peace is not a destination, an acquisition. It is an excavation. Unearth your peace. It is not foreign. It is a treasure in your bones, humming, weaving, waiting. Inner peace work need not be like bobbing for apples. No dunking, lunging, or flailing is required. Just eat the apple. Deep Loving inhale. Deep Loving exhale. Release your whole life. Recalibrate. Fill with Love and gratitude. Welcome to peace.

You cannot do your way to peace. Peace is an undoing. Undo you. Catching peace is not like catching fish or a cold. To catch peace, you have to let go. Peace is not catch and release. It is release and catch. Release everything. Catch peace.

It is a matter of space and flow, of river and sky. Peace fits better when you open your heart. Peace is when your heart says to your soul: *I Love what you've done with the place.* Peace is personal care. Sometimes you mist yourself with fragrance and essential oils. Now, go and peace yourself.

Do not confuse your need for peace as a desire for distraction. Peace is your palate. When you feed that appetite, your life calms into an ocean of grace, and spreads a light that pleases anyone who cares for you to be at peace.

Inner peace is the root of social harmony. We cannot expect a soul at war with itself to participate in world peace. Inner suffering is motivated to share its suffering. It has no healing to offer the human tribe. The work of nations and cultures for collective justice and human sacredness is the work of inner peace. If we want human healing, we must have the medicine of souls. Inner peace births collective human peace. Inner peace is necessary before peace on earth can be possible. Inner peace is the great work of our era. It is time to heal.

Plant your seeds of peace continuously. Without deeply feeling and affirming your divine wholeness, you spend life in an anxious grasping for missing pieces. You have no missing piece. Know this and you shall know peace.

Practice being at peace for one moment, then two, then a week, a month, a year. A lifetime of peace is the fruit of practice. Practice not wanting. Contentment is a dearly underappreciated root of peace.

Peace is where the soul resides. Don't leave your soul homeless. Live in peace. You don't gather peace into your soul. You let it flower from there. Its seed was always in you. Peace is a blooming thing. You cannot catch it. You have to feed it. A daily diet of Love and gratitude. Your peace will never be determined by whether someone Loves you, only by how deeply you Love yourself.

Nature's secret recipe for inner peace:
Be what you are. Be it wildly.

Peace can be shy and polite. You have to invite it to bloom in your heart. Often we are anxious seeking peace. If you can muster a flicker of peace, creating a stillness or calm, much more peace will come flooding in. It takes a spark of initial heat to start a fire. As it is with peace. It wants to join its own kind. Stillness makes the invitation.

Practice makes peace possible. Peace is a habit, as are resilience, persistence, and healing. Pause and breathe. This informs the body and mind that it is going to be all right. Believe. Faith and peace are muscles. Exercise them and they strengthen. Neglect them and they atrophy. Each repetition activates and strengthens the spirit. Peace is a weaving. Are you weaving peace? Your fingers should show the wear. Strengthen your true core, your soul. It will keep you properly aligned. In life.

Habits—including a racing mind—form from repetition. The way into a harmful habit is also the way into a helpful one. By practicing a single moment of peace, you birth more peaceful moments. Your peace bears offspring.

She birthed inner peace.
Then she raised it.

Your heart is bleating like a lamb for meadows of peace and Love's perfect water. Be a shepherd. You do not desire peace because it is foreign to you. You desire peace because you come from peace. You are weary and want to come home.

You do not suffer because of lacking. You suffer because of wanting. Wanting can be an addictive disease, a perpetual trigger for anxiety, a habitual delusion that says, *I am deprived*. Peace says, *I am whole*. To soak your bones in ultimate peace and renewal, see how long you can go without wanting. Stretch *that* muscle.

Everything you want exists, like summer just outside your unlit room. Open the door. This is how it goes with peace. When you decide to no longer thirst, you will drink the water you have always been.

Some things in life disturb you. However intense this disturbance is, a more healthful reaction can become just as intense. Practice changing the associations you have with those people and things. Sometimes even an idea causes you to suffer. This is why we struggle to have a single fruitful conversation as a society. Our ideas, our associations disturb us. This is where you can turn your mind's attention, and practice new idea connections. As you practice, your mind changes. Disturbance and peace are ultimately harvests that come from what you plant in the fertile soil of your mind.

Seeking to cure our restless souls, we go around the world, jumping from relationship to relationship. We anticipate salvation from some external place or person.

But restlessness is a stowaway. It travels with you. Wandering does not cure restlessness. It only provides new spaces for restlessness to fill. Contemplation, reflection, reckoning, daily practice. These are tonics that bring you peace. Stillness breeds stillness. Peace breeds peace. Practice what you want most, for it cannot be given to you, or found. It is in your soil, a harvested thing.

When a true yogi whispers to you, even your soul assumes a pose of peace. The key is to make all things your yogi, most of all yourself.

When you smell fresh bread coming from inside the bakery, you do not question the source. You simply go for the bread. When your soul entices you with the fragrance of peace, do not question. Go to it and eat.

What is your peace ability? You have an unlimited innate ability for peace. But under your current condition of being, what is your peace ability? How open are you to it? What are your peace narratives and are they more populous or potent than your panic narratives?

You grew up being measured by everyone. In school it was grades and scores. But as you grew, did anyone measure your peace ability? Your ability to have a meaningful, lasting peace inside? It is likely that few knew how to measure your peace ability, and that even fewer knew how to teach you to measure yourself. You may have graduated with little knowledge or skill in this. Fortunately, peace ability can always be acquired. As can your way of measuring it. You can be any age and learn peace ability. Decades of peace *inability* mean nothing when a soul is ready and determined for peace.

How often do you visit the archives of your memory and retrieve your moments of peace? How is peace to grow if it is not continuously planted? What is more a seed of peace than remembering when you were peace-full?

Your journeys have passed through all states of being. All territories of emotion and spirit. Artifacts are left over. As memories. Go. Gather your many *peaces*.

You cannot know a thing until you know a thing. As a child you might have understood someone to say, *in her peas*. Inner peace makes sense the more you long for it, then begin to give it names. Finally, you arrive, and the words *inner peace* are the ringing of a temple bell, a soothing song that melts your captivated heart.

Peace is a prophet. When you nurture real peace inside, it tells you the truth about who you are, and what this world is. Only in a state of peace do you clearly see the way forward, and what waits there.

We exercise our bodies but neglect our truest home, the soul. Buy luxuries but give away our dreams. Are easily hostile but hesitant to Love even as we yearn for it most. Want to be seen but are blind to our own truth. Pray but won't persist. Rush all the time even though peace waits for our stillness. We are the greatest paradox earth has ever seen. Which is why we are our own answer.

Finding peace is not like finding an impossible thing. Nothing magical is involved. Simply live true to your soul and liberate your Loving nature. Peace is what grows when the illusions fall away and you see clearly what is real. Which is Love.

Regardless of the conditions of your life, you can create sacred lakes and visit them faithfully. Your sacred lakes are spaces, rituals, and memories in which you immerse yourself. The immersion gifts you a moment or season of deeper peace. If you swim helplessly in the sea of how other people exist, you will become whatever that collective state is: often a state of anxiety, panic, chaos, and suffering. If you want a stability to your peace ability, have your sacred lakes. Let your heart and spirit decide.

Your sacred lake could be a butterfly drowsy on sunlight. The ointment of forgiveness. A song. Your soul smiling. Storytelling. Laughter with a friend.

Calmness

Our world suffers from an illness of anxiety: an inability to be still inside. The grand myth is that *things* must be done. Always. And yet the root of our anxiety is not that things have not been done, but that no amount of doing will ever change our essential condition: We are souls. Not the consequence of doing, but apertures of being.

We are anxious because we do not know how to be, and we can never have peace without being. We are human beings not being. Thus we suffer. Grace though is with us, for as long as we exist, we exist at the precipice of being. Being is in our nature. It is available and ours once we are finally ready to come back home. To be.

You can train your nervous system to react less to what you have previously called *stressful*. Each time such a thing occurs, remove the label stuck in your mind called *A Reason to Panic,* or, *Stressful*. You may have to work at removing these labels, as they are adhesive. Remove these labels and say to your nervous system, *I don't need you right now. You can remain at rest.* Use your own words. With practice, notice how you are less reactive. Continue like this and one day you will find yourself retaining a wonderful calm with something that in the past you would have abused yourself over.

Being calm doesn't just feel good. It opens your soul to life blessings you would otherwise miss. Calmness invites the wonders of the world to flood into your consciousness. It unleashes your gifted mind and attracts deep beauty. Spiritual insights bloom when you grow calm. Nothing wants to be near nervousness. Everything wants to be close to calmness. Attract your soul desires. Be calm.

Just when the tribe is most panicked, a river in you becomes two rivers surging. One rages with self destructive power. The other billows with peace. Crisis is a teacher who births two rivers, asking you to choose.

Calm takes practice. And your choice not to be anxious, even if others are. All day long, soothe yourself. What you want, you already are. Breathe. You're all good. Literally. You are all that is good. A calm lives in you like spring water, your companion since the beginning, waiting for you to crack open its glory and become the freedom of your original hum.

Anxiety is largely a learned behavior, often inherited from others. Because it is learned, it can be unlearned. And because it is inherited, it can be disinherited. The first step is to claim you have the power to dissolve anxiety. Claim this power until you believe in it. As you practice new life responses, you witness anxiety evaporate. Now you have a new testimony to pass on, through your way of being, blessing others to inherit your newborn calm.

One of the greatest gifts you can offer someone is your relaxed energy, the absence of your anxiety. Why would you want to offer your Lover, friend, or anyone your anxiety and nervousness? You have much more Loving gifts than those. Being fully present, with relaxed body language, facial expressions, and tone and pace of voice can be soothing to both of you, a respite from a culture out of balance. Make this your Loving practice. Give the gift that has a way of being returned to you, wondrously.

How you carry your trauma, how you care for it, and how you release it—all of this determines the energy aura you offer others. Peace is a wild animal living inside you. Anxiety, too. One needs taming, the other, to be set free.

Much of our chronic anxiety is from the phantom presence in our mind of past harm. Many times we have told ourselves, *I am not safe*. These words are a root of anxiety. Fortunately, you can choose to speak other, more divine words. When felt deeply and practiced as a daily mantra, *I am safe* is medicine that scrubs away anxiety, and reminds you of the truth. *I am safe*. A sound that sets you free.

Anxiousness is fashionable. Everyone is teaching and encouraging everyone to exist anxiously. But anxiety never solved or improved anything. It degrades everything. Don't drink that juice. Every grain of your life improves through calmness. Calmness gets into the social bloodstream and heals things. It resolves inflammation. Your calmness is an antidote. Share it.

Vaccinate yourself against this anxiety culture by breathing and staying centered in the story you are telling yourself. Don't say, *It is time to stress out*. Say, *It is time to be calm*. It is always time to be calm. Always possible. Always helpful. Everything you do anxiously, you can do calmly. And better. Anxious rushing is one of the most harmful diseases. Slow down. Breathe. Be easier on yourself. It is possible to live a full, fruitful life in a state of calm and peace.

The chronic overstaying of anxiety is very much a social conditioning and inheritance. What seems like it just appeared was present all along, primed and waiting, rooted in the genetic artifact of our ancestral and familial anxiety and trauma. These are the roots for you to touch.

Anxiety is a pollen released by fear's flower in response to the idea that you do not have what you need, will not get what you need. It is a song you repeat until it lives in your bones, a song of unmet need. When this anxiety pollen grows too rampant you suffer an allergic reaction. To reduce anxiety, it helps to learn a new song, and to repeat it until it lives in your bones. This new song has simple lyrics: *I am what I need. I have what I need. I will always have what I need. I am whole. I am abundant. I am full, flowering, flowing. I am free.*

Calm is not out there, distant and taunting. It is right here, in you. In your heart ocean, your soul sky, your forest of peaceful awareness. Let your endless searching go to sleep. Wake up inside your infinite territory, your true sanctuary. Believe that calm lives in you. It is not a myth. It is real. Learn its location, visit often. Soon you will know the way even on moonless nights. Let calm be a harvest you feast on and offer the world.

––––––––

She had always told herself she was a drought, a thing that did not have what it needed. She lived in anxiety and despair. She was a self fulfilling prophecy. Then one day she told herself she was a flood, a divine plenitude. Rains came. Beauty blossomed in her life, including most of all the wondrous flower of peace.

Breathe

When was the last time you took an entire breath? The kind that fills every cell with oxygen and life. How you breathe is a reflection of how you live. If you practice breathing entirely, you can achieve an entire life.

Sometimes, a deep breath is the biggest step you can take in the moment. Breaking your path down into simple steps can be empowering. Each relaxed breath is a healing breath, a form of self Love.

She gave herself a single self Loving mission:
Breathe beautifully today.

What a privilege to take a breath. You change the world every time you breathe. Your very words are holy water, your life the ministry. You either breathe peace into the world, or panic.

A single deep breath blesses your entire life. Imagine what a life of deep breathing can do. With one deep, Loving breath after another, you can heal your whole life. If self care is a tree, breathing is the roots. If you can breathe, you are a healer.

When the pain is severe and you feel you are dying, take a deep breath, and Love yourself to life. Your next breath is always your most precious one. A new chance to breathe better than before, to undo your knots and generations of tension.

Do not be afraid to excuse yourself from the circus and take big, beautiful breaths. Breathe deeply, beautifully. Make your breath a prayer, a rejoicing, a reunion with your life. Your breath is your healer. Your calmer. Your renewer, reminder, revealer. Your Lover. Breathe.

Breathe as if you are the sky
and every breeze belongs to you.

Don't be stingy with your breathing. Take the whole sky. Give it all back. Breathe away what is heavy. Let it evaporate into the lightness of sky. When you breathe, swallow the whole sky. Peacefully. Then exhale the whole sky back. Lovingly.

When you breathe freely, you are saying to your soul and cells, *Come alive.* Restrict your breathing and you are inviting your being to die. Gradually or swiftly, it will get to where you ask it to go. When you hold your stomach in while you breathe, you trigger your mind into thinking something is wrong. Alarmed, it releases stress hormones. By not inflating your belly when you inhale, you are telling your body, *Stress out*. To actually get stress out, free your belly when you breathe.

With every liberated breath you deepen your practice. You learn freedom. You dissolve your oppression of your soul. Entire oceans of tension want out of you. Deep breathing is the escape hatch. Skies full of peace want inside you. Deep breathing is the invitation. The window. The compassionate host.

Each breath can be a meditation, vacation, retreat, and sabbatical, all at once. Lightness of being, a state of ease, is a life skill, each breath a harvest. Contemplation is a well you visit whose water is fresh. Pure. Untouched. When you drink this water, your mind becomes fresh. Pure. Untouched. What roams through your mentality is a vapor ushered away by gently recognizing, then letting go. Sky is a canvas. Endless and renewable. So is the mind. A linen freedom woven in threads of breeze.

Restfulness

Have you ever watched the sky sleep? It gives itself completely to itself. Listen closely. Sky breathes differently when it is sleeping. It has turned its energy inward. No guilt or anxiety. In sleep, it breathes as animals breathe. Entirely devoted.

Rest is one of your most powerful medicines. It is also a skill. A habit of giving yourself permission. Do you feel guilty when you are not working yourself to death? Who has planted these seeds in you that gravely mis-define life? *I deserve and am blessed by rest*. This mantra can dissolve the adhesions of guilt keeping you from feeding yourself sleep and repose. Rest is a feeding. How would you feel if you did not feed your starving child or animal? Feel this way about not feeding yourself rest. You are designed to run on rest, before even food and water. Before son and daughter. Before Lover and labor. Rest.

Seeds have been planted in you, in all of us. Seeds that say, *You must not rest. Rest is for the lazy, the selfish, the impoverished.* Women are often most harshly judged and scolded away from giving themselves rest. You are never giving just yourself rest. Any rest you experience is always for every single person in your life. Remember this. If you feed yourself, you feed all. Not resting abuses your brain, body, and heart. Your relationships and work. Your life. Deep rest brings you closer to your original, natural state. Your optimal existence.

Try this ancient remedy:
When you are tired, rest.

Do not deprive yourself of the very foundation of your health. Give yourself permission to rest. Weariness closes the heart and inflames your prejudice. War and conflict have roots in fatigue and the inflammation of exhaustion. Sleep and rest are profound medicines. Our world is sick with tiredness. It is time for a new cultural value. Rather than work yourself to death, renew yourself into life.

The brain heals during deep sleep. Be compassionate. Let it rest. When you gift your brain true sleep, wonders happen. Trauma heals. Memories are sealed. Inspiration is seeded. Mood is massaged. Learning flowers. Chemicals are balanced. Stress, anxiety, and toxins are flushed. Beauty vision revives. Cells regenerate. Nerve pathways bloom. Peace roams and gathers all its favorite thoughts. Spirit settles. Soul drinks silence and breathes again. You wake into your true nature. Renewed. Rest up. You have many births ahead of you.

Being Present

Be present with what you care about. Otherwise, you hurt what you care about. Who would want to be in a relationship with someone who isn't truly present? If you want someone to listen to you perfectly, to understand you completely, and to be sensitive and honoring to your nature, learn to be your most attentive audience. Tune into you. Be the one. If you cannot be present even for yourself, how can you truly be available for another?

When you slow down, breathe, and gaze your soul in the present moment, free of judgment, you create an intimacy that releases old tension, dissolves false ideas, nurtures your tenderness, and reveals your true, divine beauty. This is how you heal. Not by running away from yourself, but by jumping in.

Somewhere in you is a candle meant to illuminate this very moment. Light your attention. Yearn for this moment while you have it. Of all the stories you tell yourself, get the one about this moment right. If you are not paying attention, you may see things that are not there, and later remember things that did not happen. Now is your greatest chance to see *now* clearly. Look into it.

You cannot be entirely alive if you are not entirely present. Inhabit your life. Be aware. This is living. Your wealth is not in the next moment. It is in this one. Search the right soil. Beyond doing is an endless sky of being, of bliss. If you want peace, *be* there.

In every beehive is always one who decides to stop laboring and taste the honey. Be that one. If it has happened, it has meaning. If it has meaning, it is pregnant with purpose. If purposeful, be present. For what happens next.

The most basic form of care is to simply pay attention. This is one of your most Loving acts. Care enough to be still, be present, and tune in. This is how you honor a living thing. Including yourself. Being fully present and listening compassionately speaks volumes that words cannot reach. It is your most powerful form of speech.

Walk into the woods of this moment and find the clearing where sunlight comes through. Taste your moments as they come forth bursting from the great tree of existence. Taste them all.

Here, in this present moment, is everything real. There, everywhere else, is the landscape of worries and fear. Here, is a garden. There, a desolation where peace goes to die. All the miracles happen right now. Let right now be good enough for you. It is such a present to be present in the presence of the present.

Nature of Time

All of time is now. It is fashionable these days to talk about living in the present, as though the past and future are not real. Your ancestors knew that past and future are very real, but not along some distant linear path. Right here and now. It is all happening now. If you cut your finger yesterday, the wound you have today does not become unreal simply because yesterday was yesterday. Yesterday is alive in you today, in the wound, and in its healing.

Time does not exist. No parade moving from the past to the present to the future. Just because one culture exists in an unnatural linearity does not mean you must. You can live as we always have. With all of time happening at once. This leaves you with no time at all, freeing you from the tyranny of time. The past and the future are alive right here in your present. You are touched by each at all times. Touch each with every breath.

Your ancestors are only real if you experience time in a circle, or sacred hoop. Otherwise, you only remember them, you do not live with them. The same is true with your descendants. Not just your blood children, but all living things that come after you. People who experience time as linear destroy the world because they do not experience their descendants as real, only as a linear fabrication. They have no true feeling of responsibility of caring for the earth, of leaving it well for the later ones.

In the instantaneous existence of true life, all is real, including dreams and intuition. All occurs within the circle of life. All dimensions. All times. All as real and now as the air you breathe and your body. Nothing is *once was* or *will be*. All just *IS*.

The moments aren't just going by. They are begging you to pour all that you are into them. That's what moments are: holding spaces for meaning. In return, moments give you life. Be in the water. Feel everything that has been, is, and will be. Feel it, and you will honor it. Honor it, and you release yourself from suffering. You find your peace.

Caring for Your Mind

Because your mind is a finely tuned miracle, an instrument of grace, when it is asked to process a false reality, it reacts allergically. It falls out of tune. This is how you lose your mental health. Mental health is not a tale of two kinds: a population of ill people and well people. Rather, it is a capacity for rebellion. A power living in you that directs you away from harm to you and others, and that calls you to wherever the sky and water and earth are clean. You need rivers of tears to wash out your pollution. These rivers are your mental health.

Learning to call depression by its soulful names is also mental health. Depression, regardless of its biological nature, can also be regarded as a powerful sensitivity to the toxins of this world. This is not to say depression is to be desired. Depression is an indicator, a voice, a painful kindness forcing you to attend to who you truly are. You are shamed for your depression. If you can find your kindred tribe, together you can hunt down the shame and put it to sleep.

The world has lied to you. No such thing exists as mentally ill people on the one hand and *normal* people on the other. We are all forever wrestling with our mental health. To be alive is a mental occupation, a striving against the harm of ideas, moments, and memories, an urgency toward mental peace and clarity. You will never be mentally abnormal. Mental normalcy is nonexistent. Everyone is swimming in a water of rapids and riptides and swirling currents.

All minds are atmospheres, skies of continuous change. Your mental health is your personal art project. Your sacred architectural enterprise. If you are a clown, it is good to embrace your *clownship*. Too many minds suffer trying to be more appealing to the masses. All masses are but single souls caught in morasses, molasses of acceptance and belonging. No human crowd knows entirely what it wants, only what it fears. You can run with a crowd and feel lonelier than ever. You can run with your soul and feel an infinite companionship. The way sunlight makes daytime feel.

Despair and depression are products of the mind. Uncared for minds are more vulnerable. Seeing falsely and believing falsely takes a toll. When truth seems to have fled, you can develop ways to bring it back. Quiet reflection and creative expression are mating calls for truth. When you summon what your soul has to say, clouds part. Truth comes streaming in like sun bars.

If your thoughts about yourself are not Love poems, you need a new editor. Keep your positive mental verses. Publish a lifetime of peace. A positive thought baptizes the spirit. Go down to the river. Water your Loving thoughts. Watch them bloom and water you.

What you feel is low self esteem may be high self neglect. Dwelling on your suffering is not the same thing as spending time healing and growing. Feeling down about yourself? Don't seek compliments. Seek your compassion. Help somebody. Let your Love for them gush out. As it comes through you, it restores you.

When hurt carries you to the critical edge, you may feel shame at the idea of seeking help. Seek help anyway. Bear your discomfort and find somebody. When we are in despair, we lose perspective. Our own judgment fails us. Reach out. Even a stranger can have the perspective you need, or know the next step to take. This is what matters: finding a way to move forward Lovingly. Like stepping gingerly from lily pad to lily pad, staying afloat. Let someone help you find your footing.

Lift your precious spirit. It belongs at the divine altitude of unconditional Love. Heaviness and sadness can grow to seem like your true home. They are not. Your home is peace. The air is light and fresh up there. If necessary, reacquaint yourself. The way home? Big, beautiful breaths and heaps of gratitude. Welcome home.

Much mental unwellness results from the condition of our heart and soul. You can miss the root when you treat your mind without treating the life of your heart and soul in the world. Do not abandon yourself. Start with your mind. Purify. Shed your old ideas. Your thoughts make your life. Work that garden. Thoughts are intrinsic medicine. Dose yourself faithfully.

Sadness is a vortex. Take care not to fall into someone else's. In the social world, sadness is contagious. People compete with each other over who is sadder, who has the more miserable life, who has Love abandoned more. A strange satisfaction may invade you when you digest this group sadness. Addicted, it becomes your fix. Watch closely. Are you drawn toward sad songs and images? Why? Do they feed you? Or are they seducing you into a deeper sadness than what you already carry?

Wanting to belong to a sad tribe is common. Belonging has a strong pull. If you come to a place where you want sadness no longer, you have power. You can stop drinking from sad fountains, reading sad words, listening to sad songs, living a life of sadness. You can dare a way of life called joy.

Sadness can be an addiction. Dwell in it often enough and the familiarity of it gives you a painful high more appealing to you than your unfamiliarity with joy and lightness. Like all unnatural highs, you crash. Staying in sadness, you become a creature of the sadness forest. You learn its features and roam there. Other sadness creatures call out to you, greet you. You embrace each other. In sadness. To escape this forest, you must be willing to say goodbye to your sadness tribe.

Attention breeds things. What you feed becomes your life. Water what serves your soul. Planting thoughts in your soul is like planting seeds in soil. With care and patience, a harvest soon will come. Dare a positive thought. Midwife your own peace.

When you do not care for your mind, it becomes a storm battering the tree where your thoughts come to sit. Your thought-birds screech and scatter, disturbed by your turbulence. When your mind grows still, your thought-birds are still with you, though now they grow calm and settle in the tree branches. Like this, they are free to sing lightly, and to breed new, healthier thought-birds.

She bookmarked her self Loving thoughts.
Then she wore out those pages.

Make sure your thoughts are authentically yours. When you think organic thoughts, not foreign to your soul, all your perfect music finds you. Learn to live in harmony with your thoughts and you change your life and the world. A good thought blesses mind, body, soul, and community with infinite medicine. Radicalize your thoughts. Don't let your mind lead you into slavery. Think yourself to freedom.

The heart does not cause us pain. The mind does. Love is divine and without fault. The mind runs us through forests of truth and illusion. Come to rest in the clearing where Love flowers wildly and you can see clearly.

When you begin having a negative thought, you can stop it. What an amazing power. You can host your own intervention. Learn to interrupt your false thoughts and record your true ones. Keep a master vault.

Inside the mind, planting and harvesting are happening all at once. To change your life, plant new seeds. If no beauty lives in your thought, choose a new thought. If no garden grows in your life, start planting. If you want peace, stop wanting. Hygiene includes your mind and heart. Bathe. Purify. Release. Take off your heavy mental clothes. Enjoy a springtime of your soul.

Solitude

When you neglect the universe inside you, that universe does not fade away. You do. Solitude is not the absence of company. It offers the full, undiluted presence of a divine company. In your solitude your soul expands, like a forest swelled with rain. Everything living in your soul rejoices at this pure touch of you in a moment of being.

The world shames you into feeling you are no more than a barnacle attached to others. I see how you have been scalded by this lie, this endless battering of your sense of wholeness by the idea that you exist solely to be an appendage of someone else. You are left bereft and grieving of your own soul. The integrity of your wholeness is shattered. Shame comes flooding in. Shame at not being in a relationship. Shame at being divorced. Shame at the idea of leaving a relationship that is killing you. Shame is a great shackle people use to own you. To siphon your power into their sickness.

If the idea of being single shames you, you have lost your selfhood, which is a foundation of your womanhood. Do you feel shame at eating out alone? Traveling alone? Doing anything alone? Do you feel eyes on you, judging you? They are. Judging you. Truly though, they are judging themselves. You exist in a tribe of people who have been conditioned to reject their selfhood, their solitude, their freedom.

If you offer an animal in a cage a way out of the cage, yet the animal is so terrified of the solitude of freedom that it stays in the cage, that animal is no longer its natural self. It has become a slave: to its fears more than to its master. At some point, the master is a phantom presence. What is real in the heart of a cage animal is fear. If you are terrified of solitude, you are as a child lost in the wilderness, afraid to be lost, afraid to go home.

Daughter, the way to kill shame is to grow Love for yourself. Love does not abide shame. Darkness cannot live inside sunlight, for sunlight is absolute. Shame cannot live inside Love, for Love is an overwhelming radiance of freedom.

Pride is not the opposite of shame. It is its own mutation of Love, and just as destructive as shame. If you react to shame by being prideful, you have only further dimmed your Love.

You are not an appendage. Not a part of someone. You exist as a divine phenomenon. One that can breathe, and Love, and thrive all on its own. Not that you need to seek aloneness. But that you live in the freedom of knowing your aloneness is not a crime, not an inferiority. This story has been planted deep in you. You may believe you do not carry it. Be assured, it is there.

Maybe you have dug far into yourself and found this fable, uprooted it with a fervor. Or you may still be avoiding it—this story that says you must feel shame for your unattached existence, your incomplete self. Your Love for you is not Love without the shedding of these false roots of shame. Find your sister circles and work through your shame together. Kinship empowers a soul. Truth sharing is an ointment profound in its potency. Speak of your shame. Let the air have it and testimony carry it away.

Loneliness is a paradox. We seek to relieve it by filling our lives with people, activity, and things. But loneliness is mostly the soul wanting itself. The more you abandon your soul by chasing what is not your soul, the more you invite loneliness.

Do not depend on your social world to cure your loneliness. Relationships can feed you, though only if you are also feeding yourself. I Love seeing you truly feeding yourself. I can feel your soul purring. Keep it purring. You know your native diet. You know what makes you dissolve sweetly, and all your tension run away. I don't mean your escape routes. I mean your trails running back to you. Keep moving back to you. You don't feel lonely because you need people. You feel lonely because, even having people, you ache, still in need of your soul.

Until you stop telling yourself, *I am alone*, you can never fully experience your own presence. Loneliness has little to do with other people and much to do with not learning to be at peace with your own existence.

I have seen you suffer simply from being away from yourself too long. Finally, you take a step in your direction. Instantly, out of the valley comes a stranger, ragged and smiling. Open up your door. Let yourself in.

Be willing not to be available. Shed the guilt until guilt stays away. It is okay to tell the world, *I am taking time for something very sacred. I am birthing myself once more.*

Who are you to require an audience to your life? You were created in the private mystery of a miracle. Be content to exist. Yes, even in solitude. Especially in solitude. For that was how you began. It was when you were most present and fulfilled. Know that peace again.

Inside of you is a garden. A profound inner reality. Spend your life there. Nurture it. Know where your shade trees grow. Your favorite fragrant flowers. A clear brook runs through, rhythmic and calming. Sip its blessings. Become familiar with your resting places: soft moss, bright clearings. Places of nectar and dew. Parts of your interior are filled with birdsong. Others with reminders of what you came here for. Live a rich and continuous inner life. It will make this outer world a more beautiful dream.

When was the last time you visited yourself? Your shade spots and remote nooks of soul. The tiny growth sprouts still vulnerable. Artifacts left by your ancestors that you could really use right now. Deep pools of fear ready to evaporate if only you would wade in. Light shafts of hope. Mineral rivers. Dream flowers. Memories whispered by your nostalgic heart. Old songs, new notes, tender terrain. Truth. Your truth, grazing patiently, muscles taut and aching to run. Maybe now is a good time. Go to you. Stay awhile. Harvest your goods.

Soulful emptiness is not absence but the presence of Presence. It is not lacking, but the pinnacle of having. Not poverty but the holding place for true wealth. In emptiness, stripped of identity, ego, and longing, you dilate into an openness that invites the breath of serenity to saturate your soul.

Have you truly met yourself? Silence and solitude can make the introduction. Discover the divine altitude of solitude, which is a plenitude, a multitude.

What bliss when you feel free to say to others: *Do not look for me in the market, bartering in clouds of confusion over things that do not exist. I am on my knees in the soul garden, where truth sings and flowers and flows, and has its eternal way with me.*

Cherishing Your Privacy

If you set your favorite clothes outside, soon they will be covered in dust, pollen, and bird offerings. Sun will bleach them. Bacteria will dine. The elements will have their way. The essence of your favorite clothes will be eroded until only rags remain. This is what happens to your soul without privacy. When you expose your personal life to the entire world, you invite the entire world to pollute your personal life. And it does. Not always from malice or spite. Wind carries things. What you set out in the wind becomes what the wind carries.

If you wish to have a say in the state of your heart and soul, of your journey and relationships, privacy is of value. A private life is a greenhouse, an insulated space fertile and nurturing of the things you care about. Inside your privacy, you can see things clearly and without the delusions and illusions others pass on. Your life seeds and tender sprouts need a careful touch. They can succumb to toxins and rough touches. Your privacy is their shelter.

If you care to grow new habits, new ways, privacy is your incubator. It gives new things in your life a chance to mature and strengthen. When you need to heal, privacy allows for peace and quiet, and your controlled infusion of positive energy.

Privacy is not secrecy. Secrecy can be manipulative and fearful. Privacy is how you honor your truth and the shaping of your story. You need time with your own clay. Privacy is unafraid. Devoted to sacredness. It values things, holds them in Love's light, and makes its own choices about what and when and how to share.

In some people, you can clearly see evidence of their lack of privacy. They have no center, no anchor, no integrity of being. They are filled with and exude whatever streams into them. It is difficult to trust such people, as they can be unreliable even to themselves. They easily lose track of who they are, filled with the detritus of others. Their selfness is diluted and diffused.

If you share everything with everyone, everything you are gets touched by everyone. When you go to touch what you have shared, you are no longer touching your truth. If you give away your privacy, you give away your story. Others get their hands on it and weave in new strands, taking out original weavings.

Privacy, then, is how you create the atmosphere by which others relate to you. Your privacy is a message about how you wish to be treated. When you share from a healthy private life, others tend to be more honoring of what you share. Privacy is your oasis for retreat and renewal. Your purification bath. Privacy is a vital root of wellness. I hope you will treat it as a priority in your life. Your privacy will always prioritize you.

Don't be fooled by the anxious herd's rush to make everything public. Your private life is a sacred womb birthing sacred things. No comparison or parading necessary. Keep your intimacy. Your soul swims there. Have faith in your private life. It is good enough.

If you share everything publically, you erode the soil of the *sacred personal* from which your many seeds of truth and beauty sprout and grow. Though it may not be in style, having a private life creates a cradle of intimacy, a sanctuary for pure healing, growing, being. Your life is not performance art. It is the sacredness of the soul.

Quietude

Silence is not the absence of sound. It is the sound of your soul. When you let your soul sing *a cappella*, its music washes you into a restful peace, a renewal by reunion, a sweet symphony with all things. Let all the noise fall away for a merciful moment. Let silence play.

Quiet is a symphony of truth. A window into the realm of *unfabricated* things. Species of spirit fly freely in the wilderness of quiet. You are composed of these species. You can fly with them, if you are quiet, if you let go of your anxious grip on life and learn to be with it. Quiet is an atmosphere, an ecology. A weather. Life is in quiet, comes from it. Quiet is not the stopping or smothering of things. It is an awakening. An ushering. A liberation.

Don't be afraid of silence.
It's where you find your song.

Silence may be the most powerful mantra of all. Speak it often, and your life changes into peace. Spend time in the garden of your silence. Much beauty and discovery wait there. You won't believe the blossoms.

Silence is a song deep in the soul. Let the divine music play. Your soul without silence is a symphony without music. Are you scattered? Distraction is unknown to silence. This is why silence gives birth to song. If you grow quiet, your soul becomes a song. When it grows quiet enough inside, the soul sings and truth arrives, a wondrous aching memory.

The old women who braid sweetgrass under the plum evening sky are accustomed to silence. They know it is better to weave sacredness quietly than to speak out of anxiousness, unraveling peace.

Growing comfortable with silence is like growing comfortable with the dark. At first it may seem foreign, unnatural, and as though you cannot see. Then, gradually, you develop a vision for silence. The soul opens, and truth begins to appear. At first, you can make out only a vague sense of things. In time, you see more clearly than you do in the presence of noise. Now you see through the veil of this world into the world of all that is. This clarity brings you peace. From this time forward, silence is a craving and your life is the feast.

Silence is a heavenly garden few visit.
If you go, you can have it all to yourself.

Is quiet boring to you? Is quiet itself boring, or are you relating to quiet in a way that leaves you feeling bored? By bored, do you really mean anxious? Search your mind and its associations between feelings, thoughts, and words. Many wild, wondrous things live in quiet. If you have trouble recognizing them, you can learn to see. Anything that brings you back to yourself is good medicine. Quiet can be one of those.

When you feel bored, this is the discomfort of being with yourself. Stay in this bath of anxiousness until you release from your external addictions. When you first settle into a bath, the water feels too hot. It isn't. You are experiencing the difference between your body temperature and the water temperature. As the two temperatures merge, you grow comfortable in the water. Then relaxed and purring.

When faced with the contrasting energy states of your agitated, overstimulated self and the calm of your soul, you say, *I'm bored*. You aren't bored. You just aren't used to being with yourself, in your own soul water. Stay with the feeling, don't run from it. Keep sinking down into your bath. The discomfort will pass. Your energy will begin to match your soul's natural calm. You will feel yourself relax. You might even start purring peace.

When you feel bored, instead of saying, *I'm bored*, try saying, *I don't like being with myself*. The truth of this may jar you into looking at your relationship with yourself. Quietude is not a dungeon. It is a valley. Your peace grazes there.

All this constant noise and stimulus has us anxious and burned out. The remedy for a thing is not more of the same thing. Let go of noise and stimulus. Even for a moment. Relieve your tension. Growing quiet is a massage for the soul. The absence of noise and distraction can bless you with the presence of your own presence. If you haven't met your true self yet, you are in for an awesome wonder. And if you have, you know you are waiting for you, and the divine music you are.

When you bathe in silence, you feel a familiar presence. This is because silence births every single thing. It is the womb of all that is. The more time you spend in silence, the more it becomes familiar, comfortable, safe, a friend. The more you become aware of the constant presence of all that you are, all that you need, sacred and divine.

Silence was your first language. Its tongue, your perfect poetry. All else is a translation of genius. Thirsting for meaning, drink a silence song. When you go home to your quietude, what waits there for you says nothing. Says everything. Find eternity inside its soundless hum.

Listen. Silence is teaching, and your soul is a newborn aching to know. Silence is a road your soul follows to remember itself. Your soul is whispering all you need to know. Quiet now. No more words. Let Love speak for you. Soul speaks in a pure language without words, in a tongue of silence. To hear its wondrous voice clearly, grow silent, too.

As you open up into silence, thought and judgment flutter, then fall away. A strong presence begins to reveal itself. If you keep opening, it takes you. Peace flows now, a thing like clear sky. Opening further, you hear Creation's soundless music. It comes from everywhere. It comes from you. You palm clear water to drink. This water, palm, drinking, all of it, is your boundless gathered soul.

What the mind does with silence is extraordinary. It heals itself. Purges, cleanses, rewires. We struggle in this noisiest of times for a reason. Our brains were designed for continuous self repair. The instrument is silence. Inner silence is the soul's breath. Silence in the world around us is Creation's breath. Many things are going extinct in the world and in people's lives. Preserve your precious silence.

You don't need long stretches of silence to create enduring peace. A few moments at a time can become a habit that seeps out until it becomes your life. A few moments can produce the most priceless music of peace and companionship. You can discover more wonders in a day of silence than in a year of travel. The only ones who believe this have spent a day in silence. Let go of thoughts and words. An endless sky of being waits for you. A speechless kind of Love.

Life is a beautiful paradox. Only when you are empty are you filled. Only broken are you made whole. Only in quietude does your soul sing its truest song. Inside of every silence is a wonderful sound. Within every sound is a surreal silence. Make your peace with all of it. Light the candle flaming in the hush. Illuminate your soul.

Silence is a power source for your soul, a midwife gifted at helping you birth peace. Make sure to feed your soul plenty of inner silence, one of its favorite foods. Give a flower water and it blossoms. Give your soul silence and it does the same. Hear your soul say, *Give me silence and I will give you peace.*

Quiet moments and spaces are wealth divine. Enrich your life. You can recognize the truly wealthy by a certain quietude they bring. If you want clarity for your life, shed the clatter. If you grow quiet enough, you can see life's tide approaching and what the water brings you. It takes stillness and calm to be the shore. Silence is a land you cannot own. But from it you can harvest your very soul.

Nature and You

Nature is not foreign to you. *You are nature.* To spend time in nature is to spend time in yourself. If you are not used to this, encountering yourself in this form can create anxiety. Laugh at the anxiety, stay with your nature-self.

Soon, a calm arises. This is you happy to see you. You happy to be with you. What you touch is you. What you taste is you. What you see is you. All around you, you. *Be-you-tiful.*

Falling in Love with the natural world can renew you. First, grow still. Then see if you can remember how you felt as a child when you were flooded with awe and wonder. Stare at the moon, or the way light swims through a glass of lemon water, or the path a tear takes down a cheek, or the infinity of attraction, or the dance of willows in the wind, or a smile, or a grain of sand, or a conspiracy of clouds. Let yourself grow emotional. Many people treat such childlike feeling as a crime. If it is a crime, let it be a crime of passion.

Be a wild thing. That's what this wilderness is for. If the world feels too wild for you, it might be a good time to consider whether you have grown too tame. Live free. Maybe you are a soaring bird. Use. Your. Wings.

Many care to protect the earth, yet fail to protect themselves from their own neglect. If you are unwell as you care for life and nature, you will pour your unwellness into real streams and lands and ideas that become our collective nature-ways. When you neglect your inner land, you threaten our natural land. If your soil is not good, your seeds do not matter.

If you are a water-land-life protector, you must protect your native water-land-life, which are your body, spirit, mind, memory, and heart. Protect your inner water. Take strong care of you. We need you. Go home to yourself. Heal and build. This is your power. And our sacred seed.

However good nature feels to you, you can feel as good to yourself, for you are a natural thing. Your natural state is peace. Believe this and come home. A seed has no idea what water, sun, and earth are up to. But their touch feels promising. So it surrenders. Bow like that. Give yourself to what stirs your soul. If you surrender, your seeds of promise will grow into an awesome paradise. A beautiful life is not built. It is released.

Treat your tenderness the old way. A wound needs air to heal. Go sit on a mountain. Let sky run through your soul. Stay in the wind long enough, and you too will learn how to be free. Sky is an ocean, too. Bathe in it when you can. Harvest sunrise. Feast on sunset. Live with a belly full of light. Whatever your favorite flowers do, do that. What moon did last night to sky, do that with your Love. Do it to the world.

Look for Love's evidence and you will find it. Feel a raindrop on your skin and know you are Loved. Gaze the fine edge of a leaf. Let your soul live inside that precision and wonder. Lie in a field of wildflowers, let your aura grow indistinguishable from the other blossoms. Listen to the symphony of wilderness in the key of beauty. It is possible to create a continuous sunrise in your soul. Love is that sun. Consciousness is your horizon. To learn about joy and growing, act like the sun.

Night sky is not just something to look at. It is a prayer being spoken to us on earth. Be quiet enough to understand the words. Make your offering to nature: *Up in the high wind. Where hawks draft. I give away everything. Everything gives to me.*

Who Are You

What are you here for? The question and the answer are for your sake. And for all of life touched by you. Your Love makes you divine. Remember that. Remember yourself. This is a key to peace, healing, and freedom. When you forget who you are, you act like everyone else. Your soul is Love. Don't lose your true nature. Pronounce it out loud. Say, *I am Love.*

She wanted peace.
So she forgot all she was taught
and remembered herself.

You revisit your identity thousands of times a day, a bird cawing out *Who am I* over and again. Make sure you drop *I AM LOVE* seeds. You are not what this world says you are. You are a divine thing, immeasurable and purpose full. Become a connoisseur of you. Learn your vintage. Savor your soul. Keep coming home, daughter.

Clothed inside every cornhusk is a kernel. This is how your identity hides your truth. Peel back your springtime layers. It is time for your nakedness to be blessed by the sun. If you can succeed at being yourself, you will have achieved your greatest success.

She remembered her soul before
a lifetime of objectification. It sang.

The One Law never changes. Love *you* more. Love it all more. Blow up your heart boundaries, dissolve your identity, and when you hear the word *Love*, respond. Your name is being called. Your life is a message in a bottle, drifting on the ocean of generations. Let that message be Love.

Examine your beliefs with Love, which is truth. You may find their roots are not native to your soil, your soul. An infinite world lives beyond your ideas of who you are. Don't let your identity be a plantation keeping you from paradise. No star is as bright on earth as the shine of your soul in its truth. Your soul is brighter than a galaxy of suns. How can you not believe in your own light?

Focus on your essence. Stay there. Don't let the world pull you into a long false dream of who you are. Swim endlessly in the diaphanous ocean of your soul. Remember your calling. Don't lose sight. Stay in your soul lane. Homestead your own land. And when they ask what you do for a living, answer: *I Love.*

Learn a thousand languages of Love. Grow mute in hate. Remember what you came here for. Wipe clear the mirror and see your unblemished newborn heart. You are a sunrise. Life is playing your song.

Out beyond your idea of you, a great sun burns. Your every yearning is the light wanting to enter you, to show you what Love can do. Sit at peace in Love's sun and bake. Let yourself be burned away, burned back to your essential grace.

Be reassured. Like sea tide receding over the brilliance of sand, purpose in your life shall be revealed. Love is the only true work to do in this world. Do you Love? Then you are a Lover. Move through your pain, and you move into Love. Fall into Love, and you fall into your divine vocations: Listener. Lover. Healer. Humanizer. Peacemaker. Truth teller. Hope dealer. Light keeper. Soul worker. These are the labors the world needs most. And when they ask who you come from, have your answer: *Love sent me.*

> *She remembered being a little girl*
> *who was not afraid. She asked*
> *the little girl to teach the woman.*

Your body isn't the easiest thing to give away. Your soul is. You buried treasure in the ground when you were a child. It is time to remember what you consider a treasure. When rehabilitating the world, the first excavation is your true nature. You do not need to be empowered. You are power. See your infinite light.

If you should meet your true self in your lifetime, I pray you will recognize you and stay with you forever. Use your memory to start fires in your soul. You are made of moonlight. Act like it. Your radiance is real. Behave (as) yourself. Your soul is a night sky sowed with a million swelling moons. Gaze at your splendor. Be renewed.

If you Love yourself deeply enough, the *you* of you will leave you breathless. Human life continuously pulls you out to sea, away from yourself. Swim back. Learn you. Unlearn the false you. Practice you. See you. Solve you. Surrender to you. Sing you. Your greatest gift is you.

Your idea of you is a precious thing. Nurture it wildly. It will birth your life. Remove all the seeds planted in you that are not Love. Then you will know the truth of who you are. You were born with a Loving heart. Your life mission is to keep it. Preserve your Loving nature. It is pristine wilderness. Your greatest offering. A prayer made human. Resistance fire. Warming blanket. Everything.

If you look in the wrong mirror, you will see the wrong reflection. If you want to see the face of your soul, look in a soul mirror. Look at yourself with Love. Look into compassion, pooled endlessly in the world around you. Look into kindness, caring, forgiveness. Look into the way you feed others soulfully.

Look in the mirrors that show you the parts of you not available for public consumption. Look into the judgment-free places. The corners and nooks of privacy. This is why a private life matters. If you share everything, nothing will be untouched by judgment. Human judgment warps and contorts everything. I feel your need for a free breath, unjudged. You can find this in your privacy. In your personhood kept personal.

Look in your soul mirror continuously. Never drop your gaze. It will not fail to show your true beauty and worth, birthing peace with your untouched body and face.

Self Love is a precious act of memory. A resistance to the forgetting many wish you would do. Dance to remember. Sing to remember. Cry to clear the mirror you look into. Continuously remove the false ideas of you before they take hold and become your way of seeing.

Remember who you were before the conditioning, before the harm. Reconnect with your own wellness. Journey back to your ancestral wellness, which remains in you as clearly as your genetic expression. Somewhere in you, you know what it feels like to exist as a thriving river, a coursing freedom. With care, you can bring back this way of being. You can breathe again.

It is not what you remember, but how you remember. With poison or with medicine. Keep gathering yourself. You are a light seed and the wind has scattered you. Return and sprout. Shock the soil with the roots you push out in your delirious Love fever. Abandon poise. Grow feral. Mutate. Bloom.

Your Inner Story

Deep Love flowers only from a deeper story you tell yourself. Endlessly. The story you tell yourself births your whole life. Keep drafting. Rehabilitate your inner story. If you are harming yourself, if your inner story isn't working, plant new seeds. Tell yourself stories that heal your soul. Practice self talk soaked in honey.

By now you have told yourself a trillion stories a trillion ways. Those stories need gardening. Tend to them. Your every thought releases corresponding chemicals that flood the brain and body either with toxic inflammation or calming medicine. Choose wisely. Be willing to try new stories, especially the ones whose light and lightness frighten you.

Don't leave this life not having shared your story in an intentional way. Create things. Make Love sculptures with your relationships. Carve your soul initials into every moment. Don't fear being entirely happy. Don't fear happiness ending. Wade in, and stay in that heavenly pool.

———

She burned her lifetime of false stories. What remained was her truth. She lived in that. She lived in peace. Seeing herself in the light of her one true story, she began to Love herself again. She spent the rest of her life gathering stories that fed her Love for herself.

Your Song

Sing your song. You were conceived with a song, as a song. In a healthy journey, you are raised by women and men who care to learn your song, who know how to recognize your song. In a healthy childhood, you are nurtured into your own song, the one you are encouraged to teach us. Your song is your lifelong lifeline. Your corrective signal. Your instrument of voice, power, and determination.

If you find yourself not having the first idea as to what your song is, do not despair. Your generation is a tribe that has largely lost and now reclaims its song. You are not alone in this. And in your company, you may find hope. Together, you can revolt against your muteness, against the stealing of your song. If you spend your life reclaiming your song, we shall call you victorious. And as you practice your song, you seed and fertilize the souls of your sisters as they too seek their song.

Your song is much more than music. It is how you bring your calling into the world. It is your vibration, your ancestry, your dream vision. Your song is a warming blanket, a water gourd, a grass basket for what your people need held. Your song is your medicine, your mirror, your prayer, your answer.

When you sing your song, not false or foreign songs, you fulfill your purpose, note by note. Your song heals suffering. It is a tonic wind, a bell chime of reparation. Your song is light, landmark, flagpole. It marks the way. Your way. Our way.

Spend time considering what it costs you not to know your song, or to reject your song. To betray it. Consider what it costs the world. Poverty is not a function of illusions such as money. Poverty is a soulful trait. Your song is true currency, a doorway to past, future, present. A well water in the desert. Fresh air at the mountain peak.

Souls live now that were created to receive your song. You cannot know the grand design. You can only fulfill your duty. Sing. Let your music find who needs it. Teach us what it means to be woman in your time. In your way. You move daily over stones of prejudice. Teach us how you do this while staying true to you. We have too many stories of truth leaked out on the path. Of the vast dying of soul beauty on the plains of objectification. We need your testimony of wandering and return. Sing your song.

See your true self. Why do you feel it is hard for you to see yourself and hold that image? Is your water disturbed? Are you too unstill? Asking and answering is how you proceed. Asking and answering, within your soul, is a power. An exercise in honesty, an *unburial*.

Your true self is not a myth. Not a legend. Despite what others say, a true you exists beyond the imagination of this world. Beyond your Loved ones and their projections.

A true you is out there, in you, grazing some valley you may not have entered. For some of you, you are blessed to be very close to this true you. Cherish this. Much of the world wants to take you as woman out to the deep water and drown you. It lies to you about the existence of this valley. It misleads you as to its location. Sing yourself home.

Why does it matter that you know yourself? If you do not, you cannot be alive. If you do not, you are a hungry ghost, a suffering wraith drifting the world seeking form. Your true form is formless. Stay with this paradox. Do not run from it in fear. You are trained to be needful of and obsessed over your form. A fateful project waits. Can you will yourself into a Love affair with your formless self?

You sing songs in your sleep that pierce you with your own truth. We call these songs dreams, yet they are in fact your soul gently, patiently, guiding you to the life where you may find peace. These are songs to pay attention to, to sit with, and reflect on. Be assured, as they come to you, you know the language to translate their sweet meaning.

She knew she could birth life, including her own.
So she sang freedom. It came.

A woman is song. When you remember your true notes, your whole life is music. Remember the original song you were born as. Live undimmed. Not exaggerated or shrunken. True. Not a performance piece. Not a product. A soul. Whole. Free. Rivering through a sacred life.

Your precious heart is telling you many stories. When you listen deeply, you heal. When you listen deeply to the heart stories of others, you activate their healing. When you share your meaning, you give others a chance to share in your meaning. Meaning is a sharing fire.

Listen for the song in all living things. A union lives in that music that makes every note your home. Find the sacred song in you. Surrender to the notes. Cradle the song in you. If you nurture it, let it run wild, it will grow and cradle you. Sing, and your song will sing back to you. Music is self fulfilling. A requited Love.

Don't say you can't sing. To some soul, the very sound of you is heaven. Let Love be the music you play for the world. Behold every soul dancing to your miraculous song. Sing in the octave of Love, and watch your whole life become music. Your scattered pieces still know your song. Sing them back to you. By healing, you have a chance to end generations of pain. What a gift. Open it.

She was told to be quiet.
So she sang. And sang. And sang.

All your life a song has lived in you. You have listened to the song of other souls, and suffered. No longer. Sing your soul song. Sing yourself free. You aren't produce. You are a producer. Own your music. Stream your soul. You are a living poem. Are you listening to your own song? Affirm your own worth. That's real soul music.

They wanted her to shrink, close, be silent.
She bloomed, opened, sang.
It was her greatest Love affair.

Be like a temple bell that forever says, *No matter how hard you strike me, I will sing the pure song I was created for.* It is possible to be a tuner of souls, once you have recognized that your own soul is a musical instrument. Music is the sound your soul makes when it rubs against what it Loves. Invite someone you Love. Say, *Let's you and I go walking, into the God mist, into the eternal song our souls were strung to sing.*

———

A mother handed her daughter a yellow flower full of sun and dew. She spoke to her child softly: *For you today. From the garden. Sending you Love in the keynote of nature. See how a fire lives in the heart of a flower, a person, all living things? All are my relations. Reason for this Love song I sing.*

Your Dreams

The places you dream are the places you have already been. This is why you dream them. Search your soul for its echoes of bliss, its remembrance of peace. It will always let you know the ways you have come, how sacred moments touched you. It pronounces its yearning in the mystic face of a lake, a quiet drapery of sunlight, or the lapping song of water as you stroke its softness. The beauty you dream is the beauty you have seen. It calls for you again. Release what you hold. Be touched by what cannot be held.

You are a dream life is having. Imagine that.

Tonight, your soul will go out wandering. Whatever it brings back, turn into soul food. Your soul is not doing nothing while you dream. It is gathering blessings, hoping you will recognize them when you wake. Some mornings, when your spirit is still filled with silence and mystic wandering, lie in the dark and record the clarity night has rendered. It is important to remember what you have seen through the veil.

She dreams. Then she lives her dreams.

You are from the sky, a sky creature. This is why you dream freedom and even your tears have wings. Not all revolutions are public. Most burn in the heart, transform the mind, and birth private dreams.

Careful where you lay down your dreams. You don't want to misplace them. They can scatter from neglect. When you first wake, your dreams scatter. Go get them back. Keep them in a safe place. Your heart is a good start.

How well do you know your dreams, your immortal whispers of your soul? In your soul your dreams gather and wait. They believe in you. Believe in them. Don't let anyone persuade you to replace your dreams with theirs. Suffering comes with that bargain. Sift fear away from hope. Don't invite your nightmares into your daydreams.

Night on your skin is the scent of dreams grown to blossom. When you open your heart you are a springtime to the world. In your dreams tonight, open your tender soul wide as the sky. Prepare a place for peace. Make the invitation.

Your Passion

If you are going to smolder, you might as well burn. After the fire, new life, abundant and purified. Divine Love is in you as breath is in you. It is not for you, though. It lives for the world. To smolder is half of a life, not truly a living. Smoldering is to accept remaining inside of your potential, never reaching your promise. If you are going to burn with Love, don't hold back. Devour every soul, every single living thing. Your Love is an incense that intoxicates the whole world. Never stop burning.

If you want to share the best of who you are, like incense, you must burn. Burn with passion and purpose. Release your greatest fragrance. Be all the way alive. As long as you are alive, make sure to live. Notice what it feels like to feel alive. Practice feeling that.

And Love said, Take a deep breath, human flower.
I am going to open you the rest of the way.

You are wondrous as you live in your passion. Many live in a passion drought. Keep living in your passion monsoon. Love yourself with the same devotion you apply to the rest of your life. Love yourself with a rich romance, a passion without shame, a resistance fire.

Burn your Love and compassion as sacred wild herbs, especially where spirit ails. We need the scent of sweetgrass in our souls. Light your sacred ember. Become wildfire. Your Love burn makes the whole world new.

Your tears and laughter are useful for removing the sediment of passionless moments. Be generous with them. Run to the earthquakes that make you tremble beautifully. Kites are for flying your heart near to the sun. Set your fleet aloft daily. Go all in. Seek the deep water. Climb the peak. Love the pain away. Breathe and bloom.

Giftedness

Your giftedness causes people to act strangely around you. They are encountering something they do not understand, and never fully will. It is not their place to understand. It is their place to look at you strangely, as though staring at a new species of life. Your gift is just that. A new thing. Never before seen or categorized. Grow comfortable with people not knowing what to do with you. Be at peace with the odd glances. Smile to yourself knowing that your gift is showing.

When you covet the blessings of others, you fail to recognize and liberate your own blessings. This is a poverty of perception. A sad, self imposed deprivation. Wealth happens when you remain aware of your gifts as you move through moments. And when you share those gifts in a sensation of gratitude. Soulful wealth is a habit of being in touch with blessings that are always with you, always available to drink and share, at every occasion. This is how you become truly the life of the party.

Pluck the fruits of your giftedness when they are ripe, in their intended season. Don't let your dreams fall and decay. Your gifts will terrorize you until you embrace them. Once you surrender, your gifts surrender to you. Whatever you need to share your gifts will appear to you. People. Resources. Time and health. Clarity. Gift sharing needs you to do your part. Pour your gifts. Waiting for a door to open, you miss the floor-to-ceiling window calling out to you, *Come through me.*

Your path may be a naked sky, a chocolate earth, or inundated with butterflies. Just make sure it is your path. Honor your singularity. You wouldn't be here if your uniqueness didn't matter. Your way has never been done before. Ever. Do it your way. Spell peace in your own language. Using other people's tongue, something gets lost in translation.

You are forever greater than whatever work you do. It is crucial to keep this perspective. Many lose it. Their work becomes a giant monster towering over their helpless timidity. You are spirit. Life. You have more to give and more ways to give it, no matter how illustrious or celebrated your current work.

If you feel unappreciated, unseen, undervalued in your work, help yourself. Appreciate, see, and value *you.* Passionately. Make it your art. Enlist others in the play. The meaning of your work to you changes by the moment. Grow comfortable with examining these new meanings. What you promised yesterday, to yourself or others, is not more meaningful than what truth you feel surge through you today. Beginnings and endings need not be traumatic, life threatening. Celebrate the fullness of your emotions as you transition. As you make work decisions, stay in touch with what you promised yourself in your ardent reckonings of self Love.

Soul service is not like customer service. You are not helping someone with a task. You are giving your soul into another soul in an offering that never truly ends. I am in awe of how you do this. Be prepared for how it affects you, what needs you develop. Soul service is a kind of dying. A dying pregnant with endless births. But it is a dying. The exhaustion is real and can take you from here. Keep shedding your ego and bathing in what renews you.

Your True Names

One of the most Loving things you can do is name yourself. A thousand true names live in you. Each will set you free. You have the divine right to define and name yourself. You are not choosing these names. These names chose you long ago. Now, you are recognizing and embracing them. Gift yourself countless Loving names. Make it hard to forget who you are.

If your old name is filled with too much pain, hold it differently. Not at your center, but in your caring arms. Or, let it go. Embrace a newborn name whose water is clear and comforting. Hold this new name at your center, by your heart. Let it lead your identity caravan. You are the greatest human authority on your life you will ever know. When it comes to you, you are a genius. Trust your knowing. Take your own master class.

Your Ancestors

How well do you know your ancestors of blood and spirit? They are your family and just as real and present as those who breathe and bleed. How can you know yourself if you do not know your people's history? You are their artwork.

You come from something. Those who want to own you, to colonize you, to claim you as their child, their laborer, their commodity, they want nothing more than for you to believe and live as though you come from nothing. That you are a floating realm, a soul in limbo, desperate to belong and be affirmed. Your ancestors are the root that keeps you from blowing away in disastrous winds.

> *Your ancestors outnumber your fears.*
> *Feel your power. Feel your tribe.*

Feel that mana? That power inside? Your ancestors lived not just then, but now, for you. You are greater than you will ever know. All the people of all your people are lifting you up in spirit and Love. Your fear is a dying ash compared to that eternal fire. Not only can you do this, you were born for it. You are the ceremony, the prayer, and the answer.

You are a tribal people. Not one of your kind. All of them. Eat well from this life's goodness. Live at your peak and in your power. Bless your tribe. Remember your people. Memory is how the heart holds Love. Hear your ancestors singing, dancing, crying, praying for you. If you can hear them, you will have new life.

You are an heirloom your ancestors handed down. The consequence of ages of a very particular art. The singular sum of suffering, a sunrise in a singlet of sighs. Your soul a universe of song. Birth's radiant face.

Between sunrise and sunset is a golden prairie where you walk beside the industry of your ancestors. You bend your back and gather the sweetgrass you will offer to those who come after you. Obsidian night is a stark river of dreams you swim, that your soul may swell again with hopefulness. This is not a life you are living. It is a prayer you bring to life. Hawks above remind you that you are free. Earth beneath you is the meadow where your freedom roams.

Maybe your people picked cotton, cabbage, corn, or cauliflower. As long as you pick freedom, their labor was not in vain. Your ancestors whisper to you: *Your life is the completion of our dreams. Love yourself more deeply. Be more alive.*

You Are an Ancestor

Serve your people. You will know them by the way your heart behaves. Like a candle flame bowing toward an opening, your heart bows toward your ancestors of blood or spirit. And they to you. You were born for them. You have something only you can offer. A true offering can only be made in Love. Humble yourself and serve your people. That you have breath and life is proof of their prophecy. A soul will come to pour out its life for them. You are that one.

You are not just alive. You are an ancestor in the making. How you live becomes your message. Forever. If you do not pay attention to the footprints you leave or fail to leave, you miss a chance to imprint others with a way forward. You lose awareness of how you may lead others astray. Stay close to your ancestor nature and calling. Its spirit will guide you to do no harm, and to inspire healing with every breath. When your last breath arrives, let it be said of your life, *Bless you, for you have Loved. And in your Loving, you have granted us life after your seasons. We live now adorned in your eternal grace.*

Honor your sacred circle of generations. It isn't for throwing away, mocking, or using for propaganda. Generations are life's great dance. One thing coming from another, resembling and diverging from its source, celebrating and confounding the womb that gave it life.

Your generations are mirrors. See yourself in them and maybe gain perspective. Generations abound with explanations for why you are as you are.

Generations grace you with redemption, through the lives of your descendants. When you care for yourself, you care for your generations. How, though, do you directly care for your generations? By touching them. With your attention, remembrance, tears, hopes, and investment. Give yourself.

Daughter, you are an offering for your generations, who in turn have offered themselves for you. I hope you comprehend this dance. It isn't some soulless flailing. This dance has sacred steps, is pregnant with meaning and purpose. It goes somewhere. Leads to something. Arrogance doesn't serve this dance well. Humility does. And patience. You are not the only thing unfolding. Your generations are. Their pace is on another schedule. Breathe yourself into synchronicity. Ceremonies help you shape your dutiful way of life.

Truthfulness

Your greatest challenge in life is to be your true self. Cherish the journey, for it never ends. Life's tides drift you away. Love powered, you swim back to shore. This is your life. Your magnificent maddening chore. Your soul is an endless hunger for truth. Your only hope for peace is to feed it. Here's to your lifelong feast. If you want to see your true face, look for your reflection in clear water, which is truth. Your truth wants you. Want it back.

Being truthful and honest with others is not just for the sake of others. It is for your own. Each time you lie, you stain and soil your soul. You erect a prison that keeps you from you. If your dishonesty becomes a habit, you end up so far away from yourself the way back becomes a painful task. Dishonesty pollutes your relationships with all things. It casts an aura around you that warns others to stay away. Who can trust what they cannot know to be true? Dishonesty deprives people of seeing themselves clearly in the mirror you are meant to offer. Their image distorted, they begin to relate to you in painful ways. But your dishonesty casted their image.

Truth acts like a sacred smoke. Burns your eyes open. Be honest. Honesty is medicine. Each time you lie, you lose yourself and make your relationships a fraud, losing the intimacy that could have been.

Human beings cannot bear to look directly into the sun. Nor can we stand to stare into the truth. Its brightness overcomes us. Daughter, you can develop eyes for seeing truth. The more you look into it, the more you adapt. Soon, it will hurt to look at anything that is not truth.

Your truthfulness strips you naked of illusions and delusions. You see you more clearly. Others see you for your essence. This empowers your relationships with accuracy. Truthfulness is a habit, not a wished for thing. Practice carries you faithfully to its center, where peace grows in a sunlit clearing: inner truth and outer clarity.

Truth is a climate at first harsh to the unfamiliar soul. Once you are acclimated, it spreads through your being, a mist of peace, becomes your way and language. Your resolve and temperament. Speak the truth. It is your most flattering language.

You are not responsible for other people's comfort with your truth. Your duty is to your truth. Your life and worldly touch depend on it. Maybe you believe no one is paying attention, so why bother with being your true self. Don't you see? Your aura is an ink tattooing every soul.

Do you care more about making others feel comfortable, or avoiding them being discomforted, than you do about honoring your truth? In cultures that make comfort the highest priority, people are crippled in their ability to speak the truth. Comfort is an oppressor against truth. Your freedom and wellness require making truth a greater priority than other people's comfort. Greater even than your own comfort. Let not your heart stories, your voice, be suffocated by people's expectation that you not discomfort them. You have the right to disrupt injustice and harm. You have a duty.

Your natural Love energy, and your sincere presence, may cause people to feel fear. They may misunderstand you to be the cause of their fear, when what they truly fear is their own Loving nature. Be encouraged. Your truth can help bring others back to their tenderness, back to their nature they have abandoned. Inspire souls to reclaim their soulfulness. Your fever is good to catch.

She spoke and lived in her truth.
Her soul responded by giving her peace.

A woman undistorted from her natural state is a sunrise. She floods every living thing with life. The truth of your life is a great river, daughter. Swim with its current and not against it. As for the many rivers that are not your own, do not swim them. This, too, is peace.

The power of peace is not that it allows you to avoid the truth, but that it causes you to breathe inside the truth. Thus you are free. Being authentic with yourself is a high form of self care. A determination to stay close to the fire of your truth and not go wandering. This way, you stay warm through the coldest night.

If you are dying of thirst, but spend your energy and focus on talking about the nature of water instead of drinking water, good things will not happen. Avoid letting your tribe's confusion sweep you away from what you need. Unwell tribes often speak of surface illusions, of the river's face and not the river. This is how madness stays in the world.

When her desire to be true to herself outgrew
her desire to fit in with others, she was free.

Truth is uncivilized. Civilization is an agreement. Truth makes no agreement. It is *uneditable*. Untamable. It does not care in the way we care. It burns with a constancy we cannot fathom. Truth is a wild thing. And free.

Truth is revolutionary. In a land where many speak in rhetoric without meaning, whoever speaks truth ruptures the malaise, is cast out as heretic, unleashes the bedlam of birth. Do not be discouraged by the world's response to your light. If the reaction is strong, it may be because the need is deep. If you are rain, and the desert is baking and dying of thirst, do not avoid your rain nature in order to be accepted as fire or wind. This only deprives the desert of what you were born to bring.

Your soul is not a good place to hide. All that lives there lives nakedly. Strip naked. Lose your ego, your identity, your ideas. Let your truth clothe you. Touch earth with your bare feet, breathe with your bare breaths, feel with your bare heart, see with your bare soul. Learn to go inside your soul and release what is not real. Do this, and only Love will remain. Love your own truth more than you Love other people's ideas of you.

When all you have said becomes a saying, know you have not yet said anything. Keep saying your soul. The soul says nothing. Which is why the soul says everything. In the chaos of many confused voices, remember, truth is the clearest language of all.

Do not doubt your soul. It is the truest thing you will ever know. Do not disbelieve in yourself. You are your soul.

Therefore you are true. Truth is a safe space inside you that cannot be touched. If you do not see your truth, you are not looking. All truth is visible. Even when invisible. If you have a hard time seeing yourself, you are not looking into your truth. You can spend your life looking for complicated external ways of at last finding peace. A simpler way exists. Know your truth. Tell your truth. Live in your truth.

Fairytales

Fairytales are enchanting. But what do they enchant you into? Into expecting certain things as a woman? Into hoping for, praying for, preparing for, and waiting on certain magical endings? As parents, we share the fairytales with you that we fell in Love with when we were children. We may not realize these tales are training you. We all need to look more closely at what these stories are saying, reinforcing, celebrating, and demeaning. Daughter, as you grow into a woman or deepen your womanhood, examining your fairytales is a part of your journey. Your necessary devotion.

If real life does not happen in the way your fairytales enticed you to believe, how are you affected? Who else is affected by your expectations? Loving yourself means filtering your ideas so that what remains is in harmony with true life. Life is not a game. No agreed-upon rules exist. You cannot position pieces on a board and guarantee yourself an outcome. We struggle with this uncertainty. We suffer, grieve, blame, and resent, all because life does not operate the way we were told: No magic age when things we want happen. No guarantees of happiness based on acquiring and achieving. Life does not cause our suffering nearly as much as do our ideas about life.

No one is coming to save you. What a gift.
Otherwise, you would not save yourself.

You break into a new atmosphere of self Love when you let go of your fairytale. If you have left your fairytales behind, you may be one of the fortunate ones. Too many girls begin to die with each page of their childhood storybooks. The tales that implore little girls to depend on the external world for their happiness. We say to you from the beginning, *Wait for someone to save you. For someone to affirm your beauty. For something to happen that grants you your castle, your belonging, your dreams.*

Burn the offspring stories you have created from these early stories. Look them in the eyes and, with Love, put them out of *your* misery. Hopes and dreams are meaningful for humans. Take extreme care to not let your hopes and dreams get mixed together with lies about who you are and are not. You are not a product waiting on a shelf for someone to pick you. I will never stop saying this to you. You are greater, daughter. Greater than all lies that reduce you. You are bliss.

If you work to sever your tether to social opinion, you can break that string. An elephant can be trained to believe it is captive to a string around its ankle tied to a stake. We train girls to believe they are captive to our false ideas of them. Too many of you live your entire life not realizing you can break this flimsy string at any moment. No living thing in this world is more afflicted by blindness to its own power than a soul raised to believe it is inferior, incomplete, and dependent.

Practice truth, not illusion. Illusion is a tool of oppressors, of sick souls embargoed from their own truth and freedom. Practicing truth is discouraged in a land of fear. Especially if your truth will set you free from the ways people are used to using you. Others will applaud you for continuing to practice illusions, for your practice will keep you in the place and mindset they desire for you. A world that profits from your discomfort with your natural appearance and ways will do everything in its power to keep you uncomfortable with yourself.

The way you look in the mirror can be one of the most destructive practices of illusion. Practice seeing yourself affirmatively, and you liberate yourself from suffering. Even as you disappoint others, including other women, who want you to keep seeing unacceptable imperfection in yourself. Because they see it in themselves. Because they believe they benefit from your self rejection. In truth, they do not. They are intrinsically positioned in a web of relations. As the girls and women in their own life suffer, the tide of their own suffering increases.

Be your favorite Love story. The one you watch, read, listen to endlessly. Sip it with hot cocoa or tea. Never put it down. You are not helpless. You don't have to wait on the world. Inside of you is a true world that does not wait. It moves as a river, for it is one. How you are with this inner life makes the river clear or polluted, free or obstructed. Go deep inside yourself, clear a space, light a fire, and create your own stories. Create stories that cry and laugh and bleed and that lead not to *happily ever after* but to you being closer to, more at peace with you.

Compassion

When you eat, are you eating for the world? Do you experience your food and water as a gift allowing you to serve other lives? Or do you experience your food the way a frightened animal hoards its meal? What comes to you and through you is not for you, it is for the world. Your energy to get through the day, your inspiration and creativity, your endurance and intelligence: What a bounty you have been provided that you may provide bounty to others. People talk of *passing it on* and *giving back*. In truth, nothing is ours to pass or give. All of it is a miraculous river making its way. Our role is to graciously get out of the way.

Many people bury their true soul in so many layers of fear and pain that it is hard for you to see the divine in them. Look deeper. Not with your eyes. With the divine in you. All around you are angels wearing the masks and robes of suffering. Consider them sacred. With the heart you have been given, be a passion worker in the bright fields of Love. If you want to cause a crack in human suffering, say in the heart's language to every soul you meet: *You and I should Love each other.*

Do you ache? Help somebody. Your ache is not for you, though it may seem entirely personal. Your ache is for the world. Your body accumulates collective pain the way a rain barrel collects rain. Depersonalize your suffering. Release it by comforting another in need. Helping helps the helper.

She felt badly when she stepped on grass.
So deep was her desire
not to oppress any living thing.

I see your empathic gift. Your heart aches for the loneliness you fear in the last leaf left on an autumn tree. This sensitivity, this great caring for the feelings of life around you, is a power, a challenge. Stay close to what it means for you. Using it with care, it won't use you. An ocean of Love lives inside you. Don't walk on the shore. Swim in the water. Love is a ceremony, and you are the offering. Give yourself.

A life without compassion is a night sky empty of moonlight and starlight. It sits heavy and mortal on the soul, a burden to the world. Flood your heart with a deep, boundless caring. It will raise you up from melancholy into a bright plateau of union. You will feel like your own daylight, and joy's breeze will stay.

The tribe is cold. Where you go bring Love's fire. Everybody is gestating. Your Love is their womb. In every human interaction, be a care package to the world.

She learned to place her heart out in the sun each day. That's how she blossomed.

You caring for you is an essential element in caring for others. True self care does not degrade into a selfish egocentrism that cares little about the harm it causes others. Self care is beautiful because it blossoms into a healthy, balanced caring for others. Self Love leaves evidence. It acts to transform the world around it into its own image, beautifying all things. You may have been raised to neglect your*self*, to invest in perpetual, oppressive servitude. Self care is a rebellion against that training: mystic words that say, *I value my life.*

Be sure to wash your heart before entering public spaces, before encountering living things. Much is at stake: Generations. Don't judge unless the verdict is Love. Don't quota your hugs. Stop counting. Be known for being easily distracted for the sake of your caring.

She opened. The suffering in her closed.

No one says to a waterfall, *Maybe you shouldn't pour out so much water.* Pour out your Love. Make compassion your passion. Organize a Love rebellion in your soul. Do not live with a stuttering heart. Let it speak its Love fluently. Invite all souls to warm themselves by the fire in your heart. It gets cold out there.

Know the difference between soulful servitude and being a slave. Soul service increases your light and feeds souls. Slavery drains your life, even if you feel you are helping someone. Compassion is mutual medicine, two souls sacred dancing in the same firelight, an honoring that fills both cups.

Only when knowledge moves from the brain into the heart and soul does it transform into humble, compassionate understanding that benefits humanity. Knowledge trapped in the intellect is like fresh milk trapped in the cow that curdles and sours without ever becoming life for the calf. If you spit out the idea-seeds littering your mind and look at the world the way a mother gazes at her newborn, it will heal you.

Sometimes a shepherd invites a wolf to dinner to introduce the wolf to a new diet, thus sparing the flock. Invite misguided ones. Feed them your Love. Show them your way, speak your devotion: *Take me to suffering. There, in the weeping beauty of that soul garden, is where I will pour out my Love.*

Compassion is not separate from Love. It is Love's overflow. Be a butterfly. Pollinate endless hearts with your compassion dust. Waiting for an opening, do not close. Open. Openings come to those who abandon closing. Your soul cooks a divine stew. All that remains is for you to serve the feast. You don't have to write a Love note. You can be one. Open your miraculous heart.

Kindness

Your life is three truths: *How you treat yourself. How you treat others. How you let yourself be treated.*

An ancient duty is rooted deep within your soul. *Kindness.* You are not responsible for who drinks from your fountain, how much they drink, or what they do with the drinking. But you are preciously responsible for what you pour. Some soul is praying you will be kind to it today.

Answer the prayer. And be careful how you treat people. You are touching your own soul.

You hold a key to your whole life: *Be kind.* To you. To everyone and everything. Kindness creates the climate of your life. If you care to live in a beautiful climate that feels good to you, choose to be kind and your dream climate will arrive. If for some reason you wish to live in an unpleasant climate, choose to be unkind, and you will get what you want. Your kindness is a simple thing and up to you. You can live your life choosing reasons to be unkind. Or you can be a kindness collector, finding reasons to be kind, earning kindness rewards in return.

Maybe you believe kindness evaporates like morning dew. No. It accumulates by the molecule, to become a mountain. Kindness makes this world the way a seed makes a forest. Through a single act of infinite births.

Do not let kindness in you harden like sad sap in a dying tree. You can enrapture the whole world with your sweet flowing maple. Share your sugar. Stay alive. Suffering is how the soul moves you closer to what it needs. Kindness too can be this way. When in the presence of any living thing, share your light. Why should you be kind? Let the Love you are answer.

Today you smiled at someone
you do not know, and a thousand orchids
blossomed in a grateful heart.

Want to see a special effect? Be kind to somebody. Everybody is somebody's somebody. Treat them that way. If you are rich with peace, gift someone your peace today. Your wealth will increase. If you are poor in peace, gift someone your peace today. You will gain wealth. Everyone is trying to perfect the art of who they are. Be kind. That's your way of saying, *I Love your concept.*

If you touch a flower, you leave your oil on its petals. It leaves its pollen on your skin. No touching exists that is not mutual, not intimate. Touching matters. It is vital that you take good care of your touching, and of what you allow to touch you.

Imagine if the sun waited to see if you smiled
at it first. Shine your heavenly light.

Not rushing is a kindness. A choice not to infect someone with your anxiousness. You can make a soul shiver or sing with your slightest facial expression. If we knew how delicate the social fabric is, we would treat it with care, the way I have seen you do. How you treat people is not a game. It is your final exam.

Look around you. Animals and plants are writing masterpieces on kindness, singing songs of kindness, quietly considering each other. In kindness. It is not an act. Not your imagination. Kindness is real. An energy surging through life. Some call kindness life itself.

When you are kind to someone, you plant in both souls a seed of healing that grows for lifetimes, reforesting the world. You leave seeds of harm or healing in every soul you touch. Be mindful as you change humankind.

How you treat people is everything.
You are one of those people.
How you treat yourself means even more.

Assume everyone you meet is having a hard time. It helps to wake your compassion. If you are going to presume, presume to Love. Train your heart into this habit, and your soul will be blessed immeasurably.

You don't have to limit yourself to only one sunrise a day. Be kind to somebody. Be a sweetness. Like spring. An orange blossom. Part open your heart and sing. When people see you, make them feel safer, warmer, better about themselves. Make that your life. Mind your presence.

When you encounter a human being, you have arrived at the shore of an ocean of ancestors and all their journeys. You have crossed the threshold of a tribe who has earned its dignity. Humble yourself. Bow before sacredness.

As humans, we are a tide that does not know clearly its own power. We are confused as to our true shore. As a result, we waver and worry and wander. Practice being kind. Witness the effect of your kindness. Share the moral of your kindness story. Grow to understand the power of your tide. Imagine the shore that awaits.

Kindness is a form of poetry. Write a thousand daily verses. Be ground zero in a global epidemic of kindness. Each day, start a new outbreak. Kindness is much more than a favor. It is how the soul takes a breath. Kindness is a supreme caring for yourself.

Flock to the kindness gathered in your soul. Learn to live there. Cultivate kindness. Water the ones you Love with kindness. Loving others is not simply a kindness. It is a revolution. A sacred choice. A wildfire you choose. You leave such beautiful soul prints in the world. In every flowering field of kindness, we find your sacred art.

Caring

Many expect you to be a selfless caregiver, often to the point of self harm. What does caregiving mean to you? Spend time in this idea-garden, knees in the black soil, growing intimate. Giving care is not a selfless sacrifice. Not a one-way kindness. It is an opening. When you open, things come in, things go out. Giving care is by nature a mutuality. More than that, it is an entirety. If you submerge yourself in the river, you get wet. All over.

Caring is self care. Self care is a giving of care to others. The nature and quality of your care is what matters. How you participate in and envision it. How does it live in you? If it feels burdensome, how can you lighten its weight? These are not questions and answers for you to go running for. They are for you to grow quiet and still for, allowing them to awaken in you. Your genius for caring lives in you. Imagine this. Then feel it. Then become it. Caregiver. You were born a champion of this servitude.

Relationship

What are people for, in your life? If you feel yourself using people in a way that feels badly to you, forgive yourself and correct course. If you feel yourself being used, again be kind to yourself and make changes. You do not have to give just because someone wants to take. When people are showing you who they truly are, their beautiful soul or sickened spirit, do not interrupt. Lessons are waving at you.

Are you depending on certain people to live forever? To always be the same, treat you the same, share in your old traditions together without end or evolution? These are hints of dependence in your way of relating. Being out of touch with your dependencies creates blind needfulness that can harm all involved.

Relationships can be like caged doves. They need to be continuously set free, back into the sky. If you return to each other habitually, over days or decades, be mindful of this migration. Does it groove you with unhealthy habit, or decorate you with a rich depth of meaning?

Loving people like a boa constrictor, squeezing them to death, is not Love. Love them like sun Loves its own light. Set them free. Souls are a wild thing. As are you. If your

Love does not leave them free, it is not Love. Whatever you cherish, let it be free.

Journey with those souls capable of daily wonder, awe, tears, laughter, kindness, and compassion. They will lead you to life. Choose wisely. Not the crowd. Not the acclaim. Soul. Full. Ness. Every time. People in your life are rivers meant to carry you further into your true self. Swim that water, but stay in your current. No one has the warmth you need most. Love is your innate, immutable fire. Consider yourself warmed.

The word is *relationship*. Not *relation-drown*. Two souls together are supposed to keep each other afloat and in progress. When you feel as though you are drowning in your relationship, you have choices. You can learn to swim better. You can change the conditions of the water. You can change the nature of your life with the water. And you can get out of the water, daughter.

What if your heart was so open that all you encountered considered you to be food for its soul? Being soul food is a mutual miracle. What you feed, feeds you. Swim out into the open water of someone's beauty and want nothing. Just float. That's the best kind of Love.

You are the sun in your 'soular' system.
Believe in your light.

You are the center of your life. You don't have to orbit anyone. Imagine the sun anxiously seeking someone to brighten its day. What an awesome soul power you have. Illumination lives in you. Believe this, and your lantern performs its nature. Light up your life. Warm yourself when you need to. You aren't lacking. You are Love. When you neglect your bathing in this Love, your gravity is weak, leaving you more vulnerable to being pulled into other people's atmosphere and gravity. Staying in your atmosphere takes staying in your Love.

Each person you interact with is a chance for you to practice your Love. This makes your bond with them a practice space. Be grateful for their offering. And be sure to practice, or else your bond will just be a hollow space.

Communion is the point of all relationship. Self Love is a beginning. Union is the selfless frontier. Sharing breath, water, blood, story, and feeling. You are here for these things. To touch sunlight with your joy, to be touched by its song in return. Every life needs a garden into which it may plant its meaning and memories: Relationship.

Belonging

Your desire for belonging is in many ways your soul asking you to Love yourself. When you comprehend this, your whole life can blossom. Belonging is a powerful drive. But belonging to what? When we see people as perfect shelters and homes, we create expectations and dependencies that harm our relationship with them. We abandon our soul, which has offered our most complete and lasting belonging all along. We have vast Love to share. Imagine sharing it fully with your self. Daughters, teach each other how to move into your own souls.

If you are waiting for your family, friends, anyone, to finally, truly know you, your wait will not end. No matter how much they Love you, others have only an idea of you. An imagination. A projection. They are experiencing themselves through you, consumed within their own dream. For peace in this lifetime, surrender to your divine unknowable nature. Derive contentment from the shimmering reality that you are the only human being intended to profoundly know you. Then, blissfully go about that journey. Let at least one person in this world grasp your essence: the only person who can.

Your people will never fully know or understand you. You are too divine a universe for that. Your phenomenal soul cannot be understood. You are not here for that. You, like all phenomena, are here to be experienced. Be at peace with that. Be pledged to your own soul. How wonderful a blessing it is to be at peace with your singularity, and with other people's journey of simply beholding you, imagining you, learning you. What a gift to have such peace, and to be free.

Since birth your mind has been wailing, *I am alone and separate from all things!* While your soul has been crying out, *I am inseparable from all things!* Your mind is a dear friend, but very fickle. Your soul is an absolute fire of truth. Take your soul at its word.

All yearning is the soul saying, *Come home to me.* When you stop practicing yearning and begin to practice true belonging, you realize that yearning is not a requirement for being alive. It is an inheritance, a deeply rooted habit obscuring the truth of your union with all things and the companionship of your own soul. As this veil lifts, so too does your anxiety. Now you are the energy of contentment and peace, and new, radiant forms of belonging wash into your life.

> *Yearning for something to belong to,*
> *she realized she was that something,*
> *and she perfectly belonged.*

You have no need to chase attention. You are a continuous phenomenon of attention. Recognize your sculpture, sculpting, Sculptor. You are divine. This means you are in the hands of the most perfect attention of all.

We often think of Love in reverse. We say, *If only someone would Love me, then I would Love myself.* If you do not Love yourself, no self exists for someone to Love. Self Love is the ground from which mutual Love grows.

Sacred Love is the union, the perfect womb you want your whole life. Search no longer for your true Love. You have already won the Greatest Heart. The evidence? Your life. To be alive is to be Loved. Ponder this until it sinks into you, until you understand and believe it. The Love you want is not out in the world. It is in you. It was all along. Your soul is big enough to live in for a lifetime. Let that be your belonging. Water your own garden, then see what glory arrives.

Abandonment

Abandonment is an endless ball of yarn in you. How can you know when the first abandonment happened and to whom in your life? Abandonment is generational. Seeing it as personal diminishes your power over it, your understanding. How quickly your mind defines abandonment as a signature of your own unworthiness. Unworthiness does not exist. It is an idea we pass around. A feeling that weeds itself up in our crevasses. You cannot exist and not be worthy. Worthy of healing, of being a whole, reckoning, relating human being.

Her life began when she realized their displeasure
with her was a sign of her having Loved herself.

If you stay with your Lover, make sure you are not leaving yourself. If you leave your Lover, make sure you are staying with yourself. The same holds true with all your relations. Do not abandon yourself. This is your first and last challenge. Grow in it, and you learn how not to abandon anything else you Love.

Seeking Approval

A flower does not bloom because it hopes someone will see it and approve. It blooms because that's what it was made to do. It has a blossom inside. A certain peace gets made this way. Whatever you create in this world, do not care too much what others think. Not even family and friends. They have their own blooming to do. Free your flower. Your bloom is what your soul needs most for peace.

When you let go of pleasing others, you are freed to please your soul. Your life becomes a work of peace. Peace is not a mood. Not a conditional attitude. It is your innate nature once you learn to let go of pleasing others and begin a habit of soul fulfillment.

> *She let go of pleasing others*
> *and began to please her soul.*
> *Her life became peace.*

Even before birth we fall into a habit of accommodating others. Along the way, we can lose our truth. To find it again, gently take note when you find yourself accommodating. Practice correcting your course. Soon, your habit of being true will be the deeper habit, and you will follow it. Like a pristine river following its riverbed.

Advertising You

Do you advertise yourself? What are you selling? What do you want in return? Spend time with these truths inside you. They shape your life. It can be hard not to advertise. Being truly yourself without motive is not as easy as it may seem. Motives get into us early, before birth, when we begin learning how to communicate. Communication is a carrier of motives. By now, at your age, you have developed many layers and languages in conveying yourself.

Some of your ways are conscious, others are not. Maybe you think you are trying to draw evolved people into your life, but your behavior is attracting circus clowns. Not to say circus clowns are not evolved. They do have to deal with audiences full of clowns. Maybe they are geniuses of social insight. Maybe we should call them circus monks. Don't be distracted by my wandering.

Look closely into what you radiate and emit. What does your tone of voice advertise? Is it what you want to be advertising, if you want to sell at all? How about the way you react to stress, conflict, or disappointment? Maybe you do not wish to sell anything ever. Is this possible? Is it fruitful for you in a healthful way? Do you do things that attract unwanted attention? Can you *unattract* this kind of attention? Does this require selling yourself out, or selling yourself into your truth and wellness?

If you want to attract people who respect you, are you advertising something that appeals to people who are likely to disrespect you? What kind of Lover do you want? Does this kind of Lover have a distaste for what you are advertising or how you are selling it? Whether you should be advertising is up to your own moral judgment. But if you are advertising, at least take care that your bait is on the favored menu of what you are fishing for.

Affirmation

Sometimes all a soul needs to hear is: *I see you. I feel you. I have faith in you.* Affirmation is a most healing touch. Especially when you speak the words sincerely to yourself. Self is a soil thirsty for the rain of affirmation. What sprouts up from that softened soil? Your soul.

Validate yourself relentlessly. Resist the dehumanization and the doubt. Affirm your soul drumbeat by drumbeat, and bloom into your possible life. A tidal wave of unwellness threatens to wipe out your soul print from the glorious beach of this world. Mind your soul grains. Build your fortress. Make it more powerful than the creeping tide. Make it so powerful it colors the tide and makes that flowing beautiful.

Homefulness

Daughter, if you do not make a home within yourself, how can you ever in your life find a home? Be content and in harmony inside your soul. I call this *homefulness*. Your first home is not your mother's womb. It is your own soul, itself a room within the infinite Home that is. Many of us, when we are born, begin a gradual, often lifelong moving out of our true home, the soul.

Many forms of homelessness come upon humankind. Lack of shelter. Perhaps more epidemic, lack of peace within the soul. Homelessness of the soul is a plague of our times. For you who are hurting, may you know the utter truth that you are not alone. Love is with you. The most divine and everlasting home of all.

The homelessness we see out in the world—that many scorn instead of choosing to relate to—is a symptom of various inner homelessness. Not all of these forms are by choice. Chosen forms have to do with your relationship with you. If you are soulfully homeless when you enter a relationship, you have not brought the relationship blessings of balance and harmony. You have brought a desperation that a relationship cannot hope to resolve.

Grow your homefulness. With your body. Your scent. Your temperament. Your moods, your moon flow, your memories. Your path, your purpose, your priority. Don't be on a journey home. Be home, on a journey. Come home to yourself. You are waiting for you. Be the one who is there for you the way you always dreamed of. It can be as simple as staying home, in the soul.

Something has been calling to you all your life. Answer. You are already living in your dream home. It is called your soul. No other home more perfectly suits you. Find peace there, the only place it grows.

Many go homeless their entire lives, searching for some person or place to make it all better. All the while their only true home, the soul, goes vacated. It is late and you have no business being out. Go home.

———

A woman, an elder among her people, was overcome. She felt the warm aura of her heart seep deeper than ever into her soul, and seeds long buried stir and rupture into birth. The greatest peace she had known bloomed and rivered, leaving her awed in a weep of joy. *So this is Love,* she said. *At last, I make this home in me.*

Family

A family, by blood or spirit, is prayer whose every word is intensified. Love is intensified. Hurt and anger, too. How you define family does not matter as much as how you treat family, and how you allow family to treat you.

Great suffering unfolds in souls who tell themselves they do not have a family. Great joy flowers in those who treat life as a gathering of family. Where you find family, feed it. Offer everything you truly are. The more you nourish family, the more it becomes medicine in the world and in your life. Make family a continuous celebration of all that you cherish. Bring family your clean heart and discoveries of joy. Let family nurture you and filter out social pollution. Honor family by honoring your truth. Ideally, family is an oasis for you to learn yourself, share yourself, and become one with the larger family that is life.

Be careful how you define family. Too narrowly, and you miss true family. And when you define family broadly, be aware of your expectations for who you call family. They move along on their own imperfect road.

If you Love your family, you may have to defy their fears to live your most fulfilled life. Living beautifully, you bless your family and their Love for you. Sometimes family has trouble seeing you, for they cannot see themselves. They may not see your future, your gifts, the way you do, as they are blind to their own. Bless your family by blessing your life with self determination.

What comes with being a daughter? If you feel crushed under the weight of daughter-expectations, examine the sensation of crushing, the weight, and the expectations. Pick all of this up from the sand and, holding it in your palm, bring it close to your eyes. Behold it. What do these feelings teach you about you, about others, about the choices available to you? Daughterhood can be an oppression. And a phenomenal revelation.

Friendship

It feels good to call someone a friend. But this can leave you vulnerable to overusing the word. Are you collecting token friends to nurse your loneliness? *Friend* is not just a word. It is a living thing. An energy. If people you call friend are not truly a friend, you have created exponential imposters in your life: sneaking imposter expectations, experiences, memories, and meanings. How you define friendship may not matter as much as how able you are to recognize someone as a friend and another as not a friend.

Have you had a proverbial knife plunged in your back? Betrayal hurts. Greater than this hurt is the clarity and truth you gain about the relationship that left the knife in you. Cast your net of who you call friend too widely and many people will end up in your boat who are not a friend. As they reveal themselves, empower yourself to release them from your friendship. Not to harm them. But to clarify and lift your life.

The sweetest nectar of friendship with others flows after you have made a Love offering to yourself. Not a need offering. Become a friend to your own soul.

Friend is a word that when used preciously pulls you into safety and caring. Friendship cares more to understand you than to judge and attack you. If it does not understand you, friendship at least makes the effort. It grants you space, does not set a clock on the time passed between visits. True friendship is secure in its Love, knows that Love is the silk in the web of companionship.

Companionship

Often, our greatest yearning is for companionship. Only when we learn to embrace our own companionship do we relax into an infinite companionship with life. Too often have we trained you to believe and feel you are incomplete, less than whole, dependent on external belonging. *I'm all alone* becomes an identity mantra chanted all lifelong. Release this untruth and you fall into the truth of your perfect companion, your soul. Now your walls of fear, anxiety, and desperation dissolve, and the beauty of this Creation comes rushing in. Now you feel more belonging than ever. You are a secure, peaceful oasis for your every relationship.

Explore your sublime inner coves of soul and aura. They may lead you to paradise, the union of all living things.

Self companionship is a root in your earth for the bounty you offer to others. It is the basis for your ability to participate Lovingly in humankind.

Once she learned to wildly Love herself,
she was never lonely again.

Love yourself as a sacred blanket to keep you warm. Do not depend on others for that, even as you cherish their affection. You have many cold nights and days. You have the right to be warm, to know your blanket is there for you when life chills. Learn to build your own fire, to tend the coals, to seek its glow when you are lost. Wrap yourself in your blanket. Grow familiar with its everlasting scent. Others can always add fibers to the weaving.

Romance

Pure romance can explode your soul boundary into ecstatic union. It can be a gift of your lifetime. It deserves you moving into it with deep care. Do not burrow emotionally into another seeking escape or intoxication and call that Love. It is possession, and steals from you both what Love can be.

So often, I see you courting others, only to stop courting yourself in the process. This can leave you with nothing to offer the relationship but your neglected self. This leads to rejection. And even when you have a Lover, your Lover is left with a bouquet of your wilted flowers, your neglected self. Maybe both of you are offering neglected selves. This is a relationship of wilted flowers. The nectar and sacred water are dried and gone.

I have seen you confuse a person desiring you with the idea that you are being valued. Desire is not value. Want a Lover who wants you the way earth and sky want each other, not the way a vulture wants a carcass. If you offer up your life into the deadness a vulture wants, your offering is wonderful for the vulture. Not for you. You may take sexual ecstasy for Love and devotion. But your Lover may take it for taking you. Know the difference.

Is your Lover holding you in Love or in possession? Know the difference. Are you so terrified of being alone that you would let yourself die inside a relationship? If this is so, intervene in your life. Speak the truth of your fear to someone close to you. Once spoken, your fear can weaken and grow frail. Dance, sing, create your courage. Devote yourself to healing. Then, daughter, dare to exist.

I hope your Lover lifts you up into being you. That your relationship with your Lover washes the world's dirt from your eyes, leaving you with perfect vision for seeing you. If you wait for your Lover to change, you may miss your entire life. Expecting someone to change is a form of ownership, a perceived control. Hoping for change is a fertile energy for both of you. Always encourage your Lover to spend time gardening the soul. You can inspire your Lover by doing the same.

Don't mistake the scent and heat of a Lover's body for a Lover's soul fire that can warm you for a lifetime. No matter how beautiful, you do not live with the body or the face nearly as deeply as you live with the soul. It is the soul you choose to spend your life entwined and immersed with. Your roots growing into a tight twist. It is the soul you look at every day, share spirit with, smelling its scent, shaped by its rhythm until you are dancing to a second music. It becomes your home, culture, and reference point. Your mood, aura, tenor, and treble. The soul affects your seeing, feeling, saying, doing. It becomes an additional seasoning in your native stew.

For a river stone, water is the sky. For a true Lover, passion is only the first breath. What comes after is a breathing that does not end. Let romance frost and spice your life with grace that journeys everywhere you go.

Sexual Life

Daughter, even if no one ever sees your body, you are a sexual being. Even if you never make Love, you are still a sexual being. You do not need to be sexualized. Your sexuality does not need to be exaggerated, paraded, pronounced, or publicly marketed. Though others want to sexualize you to benefit from the soulless carcass they want you to be, you can remain free and in your sacredness. Your sexuality sweetens in privacy. How wine becomes inside grapes, it cannot become outside that intimacy. Be secure in your sexuality. Fear and insecurity cause it to leak out to others that have no business with it. They will not care for it the way you do.

Your body is for many things. It is not for bartering. If you treat it as a commodity and not a sacredness, you may reap untold suffering, for the passion sewn into you is a sap running for the sake of life and abundance. Passion does not course through you so you can acquire things and desires. When used this way it mutates from a bright river into a sludge of self harm, an erosion.

Remember, what you allow into your ceremonial cave marks the walls with its endeavors. Its spirit and intent leave their enunciation inside you. It becomes a language speaking its own tongue, aspiring for its own ends. Choose sincerity for your sacred cave. Invite what feels, and speaks, and acts truthfully.

Do your best to slow down your anxiety and fear, so you may sit beside the river of your discernment and discern. Discern whose spirit is good for your intimacy. Your intimacy, accumulated over seasons, makes you. If pure minerals seep into a mountain stream over years, the stream becomes pure and mineralized. If pollution, however slight, fouls the stream, eventually the stream becomes something that retches even at its own odor. Nothing comes to drink from it, to share in its original gift.

Daughter, you are not a landing place. Not a dumping ground. Not prey. Not a performance. Not a sacrifice. You are a ceremony, holy and inspired. Your sexuality is part of the spirit rising from the fire. It is fabric of the prayer. When you hold your sexuality sacredly, you free it. It blooms. And in freeing it, it frees you, into a wilderness within your entire wilderness. An openness of ecstasy. A discovery of how deep your waters run and flow.

When honored within true intimacy and affection, human sexuality is a beautiful thing. It can make the spirit sing. The elders of my elders have spoken this since before this land looked like this land. Sadly, we attach sexuality to our most unhealthful drives: loneliness, despair, fear, insecurity. We use it as a sedative, trying to chase nightmares away. We use it as a hunting net, desperate to catch a living thing.

If you fear your sexuality, you end up abusing it. Whether by neglect, or assault, we abuse what frightens us. Where is your Loving touch? Do you understand that your desire for another is truly desire for your soul to be fed? Do you choose a Lover capable of feeding your soul? Or is your Lover full of suffering and fear, unable to feed the self? Without self Love, how can your Lover feed your soul?

Look at us. We go running from empty well to empty well expecting water. Our thirst grows. In response, we run harder to the next empty well. We grow resentful of wells for not granting what we want. Now we have a hatred for wells even as we keep running to them. What if we learned first to fill ourselves with water? What if we learned how a well filled with water behaves? What its scent is? How its energy feels?

Discern sexuality from sexual dehumanization. The world has battered women into sexual shame forever. Some women respond with exaggerated sexuality as perceived resistance, rebellion, liberation. Pushing back against being pushed down is righteous. Be careful not to push back so hard and blindly that you end up pushing not against tyranny, but against your own sacredness.

Ego says, *I have been called these things, treated these ways. Now I am going to show them. I will call myself these things with even more passion, treat myself these same ways with even more conviction.* Many revolutionaries end up creating the same tyranny they fought against, only now they are the tyrant against their souls.

Lust has its purposes. Take care that you are not intoxicated by its perfume into believing lust is Love. Many have traveled this road. Rarely does it end well. Desire on fire is not value. It is want. It feels good to be wanted, but what are you wanted for? In the end, your precious heart and soul want to be valued, cherished.

If you are not making Love, what are you making? You are making something, you can be assured. Something real and rippling comes forth when souls weave themselves through body and breath.

Your sexual energy is meant to grow into fields of Love. To be planted and harvested for Love's sake, to beautify the world. If you give away your sexual energy carelessly, with your eyes, spraying it out flirtatiously, you will succeed in spreading it. What it grows into will be another matter. Countless reports of pain and suffering come in from the crops where sacred sexual seeds have been dropped like meaningless husks and shells.

Growing

You cannot change if you do not change. How often do we file verbal, behavioral, and emotional complaints, wanting things to change? How often do we then address this desire by changing? Effort and persistence is the frontier we often fail to reach. We fear change and doubt our ability to achieve it. What then is our way through? Sometimes we wait for the pain to be unbearable, then we believe we will change. You do not have to slingshot your way to healing.

We also use moral arguments to fuel our change. But what happens when your habits are more powerful than your morality? Morality motivates you to change, once you have already strengthened your bonds between morality and your life.

How has it worked out for you to wait on others to change before you change? Changing is the best way to change. No shortcut exists around this mountain. Begin. Be a good host for what is good for you. Pay close attention to what you choose to water. It will grow.

Perspective is an advantage of living longer. The more perspective you gather, the more you have to share with younger ones. Though they may not know it, they dearly need it from you. You have no need to be shy. If you offer it in Love's spirit, without judgment and full of warmth, they will likely receive it. We are all sucklings. When we taste the milk we need, we open.

If you use other people's measuring sticks to assess your own maturing, you may find yourself not maturing but regressing. Don't look around to see what others are doing. Look inside to see what your soul is doing. Soul doesn't do. See that, too.

A tree does not say to itself, *By age 30 I want this many leaves, to be this tall, this wide, to drop this many seeds, to know this many other trees.* It does not rush. It does not beat itself up, put itself down, doubt, or despair. A tree just grows. This is why a tree knows peace.

Many of us collectively practice a culture of big steps. We look for big steps to change our lives. We work our way up to taking big steps. We wait for the perfect time, place, and conditions for big steps. As a result, we fail to take the small steps that ultimately lead to big change. The glory of an ocean of sand dunes is not the result of big steps. The smallest, single sand grains dare take the smallest of steps. To move. To shift. To arrive over and again into their purposeful place in the phenomena of constant change.

Comparison. Impatience. Fear of growing. All of this kills your growth. Many things fertilize your growth. Your growth encourages your growth. Keep growing. Accept the smallest increments of growth. Don't lose yourself seeking the grandest fruits.

The pleasure and the problem is that in every moment of your life, you are newly born. A soil exists where you belong. Make sure you are growing there. You are on a journey. Sometimes trees and shade. Sometimes the wide, naked desert. Every moment a new paradise. Enjoy being there. Persist. Keep planting yourself in peace. It isn't the mountain that gets you. It's the steps you don't take. Keep climbing.

What an honor it is to be you. No one else will ever be given the divine assignment. Enroll in your own soul. Be your own trend of one. You are earth. Full of seeds. A paradise in progress. Let the husk of your immaturity fall away. Life is a field of grain, you have rising to do. Keep waking. None of us has arrived yet.

Sometimes the messages you receive about your life arrive to you like obvious starburst. Sometimes as a whisper more subtle than silence. Be ready. Even a blade of grass has something to teach one who is looking to learn. As you lose your hunger for drama and gain an appetite for peace, you know you are growing.

Early in its growth, sugar cane is bitter.
Wait your turn for sweetness to come.

Growing doesn't always feel good. But its fruits are most delicious. Easy now. Turn your ground. Knead your dough. Tender rise. Ease into it. It isn't impossible. It's just new. It takes time. Be patient with yourself and cherish the moments along the way. You're getting there, even when it doesn't feel like it. Be encouraged. Gently. Gently with all of it. Behave like the breath of a napping newborn. You are one. New. Born. Be patient with yourself. Each moment is your first time.

Whatever you are meant to grow into isn't going anywhere until you grow into it. No need to rush. Find your rhythm. Behave like a blossoming thing. Make a soul agreement: *I will Love myself shamelessly.*

Cherish your accomplishments, each and every seed along the way. One day, you will look back and see those seeds make up the garden that is your life. In this very moment, you are practicing something. Let it be peace.

Bloom in the pitch black night of your moments. Don't wait for sun. The glow in the dark is *you.* You were born candlelight. Live so. You belong in the sky with sunlight and stars. Rise. Claim your new identity, then you change. See yourself in a new way, then come your new ways.

Your assignment in every moment is to be reborn. Open your soul window. Love's moon is ready to enter your life and birth you again. The wind is high and your branches keep breaking. As long as you remember you are a tree, you will regrow your limbs.

To keep anything fresh, it must be renewed. Learning keeps you fresh throughout life. Once you learn to separate conditioned, obedient learning from the dance your soul does at the taste of new life, you can have a romance with learning. You can keep yourself refreshed, growing, healing, alive.

Touch things with your heart, curiously, respectfully. Be touched by things in the place where your feelings and mind meet for summits that change you forever. Keep being splayed open, ground into soil, conceived into seed, birthed into bright green forests.

Turn over the mattress of your habits and comforts. It grows worn, sunken, and hard in spots where you aren't learning. Learn for you. As a celebration that you have a brain. Learn as a way of filling up your water gourd, your harvest basket. People thirst and hunger. You have something for them, born of learning.

Learn to unlearn. Unlearn everything. Be an infant seeing all things in their miraculous shimmer. Learn grace. It has ways. Feels certain ways. In the end, you have your own knowing of grace, which births more grace. Loving yourself means you are always teaching, forever learning. The absence of teaching and learning is the presence of neglect. Neglect is not Love. Evolving is.

Your Teachers

Young daughters are swimming an unknown ocean of suffering today. We have left you confused, alone, lost, misdirected. We have told you illness is wellness, and brokenness is jewelry all the popular ones are wearing.

We have spit on morals, ethics, character, and kindness. We celebrate ugliness, hurtfulness, malice, and deceit.

Your soul knows the world is upside down. So it swims for the surface, not knowing your mind has placed the surface at the bottom and the bottom at the surface. You do not realize you are swimming down into the mud, beyond the reach of light. Find that distant glimmer to orient your direction. Wellness is not beyond your reach. You have teachers that are not human. Look to the trees, sky, water. Look how things are supposed to behave. If you choose your role models well, you will be well.

Something in your soul emits a beacon, calls forth the teachers and safe spaces that have been assigned to you. Your need is a gravity drawing them to you. In union, mutual need is fulfilled. Glory rejoices. Stay open and alive with hopefulness, that your beacon of soul desire may do its sacred work: creating perfect provision.

Maturity

What is independence but your consistent ability to live *interdependently*? If you cannot live in healthy relations with others, you cannot achieve independence. Instead, you will be in a lonely downward spiral of disconnection and distorted seeing. Only through honoring relationship can you see anything clearly: yourself, others, the world.

If you make light of the importance of harmony, you create disharmony. You either move toward one or the other. They are destinations at the end of a chosen movement. If you grow so used to disharmony that you hoard it, peace and wholeness will be a threat to you, a foreign invader that you may fight to the end. The end of your disharmony or the end of your life.

Are you practicing anger? Then you must be very good at it by now. Some celebrate righteous anger. Be careful. Practice this and you poison your body with inflammation. You can practice peace just as easily. And you will become good at peace. If you say you aren't good at peace, but haven't faithfully practiced it, you have not given peace an honest chance.

None of us has mastered our feelings, even after all these years. Be easier on your peace practice. Many beautiful things take time. Rivers. Moons. Grand canyons and towering mountains. Patience does not just relieve your anxiety. It empowers your sculpting of beauty.

The nature of what you pray to is Itself patient and peaceful. This is your standard. When you practice patience and peace, you bring the nature of your Creator, your Lighthouse into this world. Your practice is not for you, in the end. It is for all living things.

Undo the social bindings people have fastened around your identity since birth. You are not to be used. You are not a part, a fragment, an assembly of pleasure and slaved servitude. You are whole. Never break yourself up into parts. Never sell your false parts. Always be undoing the knots and ties that cannot bear your freedom. Bear your freedom. Feel the pain that comes with setting yourself free. Soon the pain will fade, and you will know real peace.

Each of you, regardless of age, wants the same thing: for your mothers or daughters to Love themselves. You can help your parents and children by showing them your own Love journey. Share it with them. Let them know what works for you, and what hasn't. Learn to laugh about it. Laughter's energy can transform your trauma.

Know that your heaviness can be enlightened. You can shift your energy. Believing this, is the birth of being a shifter. You are not doomed to wearing your heaviness like a suit of chains. You can shift steel into fluid, fluid into light. You can wear gossamer clothes. You can float. Summon your entitlement, and your power arrives.

If you want to decorate yourself in makeup, make up a true story that makes you fall deeply in Love with yourself. Apply that foundation every day. Powder your soul with it regularly. Make up into self Love. Don't make down into self rejection. Don't be trapped in a mask of illusion. Be highlighted in the nakedness of freedom.

So many contours and crevasses live in the grand canyon of your soul. Spend your life discovering these soul spaces. Knowing yourself will set you free.

Love is not possession. Learn to leave free what you have been taught to squeeze to death and you will have new life. When you let go, Love comes flooding in, and joy springs out, a fountain that sings freedom.

Bless yourself with a fresh bouquet of mental flowers every single day. All flowers begin to wilt if they have been separated from their source. Keep your thoughts rooted in the source of your truth, and your thoughts will stay fresh and full of affirming life.

Your Awakening

If you ask me how many times you may awaken, I will say take the number of sunrises in your life and multiply that by the number of lives inside of every sunrise. Your awakenings are endless. Most of them, you do not graduate from formally. As you go on living, you learn to recognize and cherish them, sublime as they may be. Never tell yourself you have reached your grand awakening, that you have no more enlightenment ahead. *Still waking*. These words create your humbling.

When the circle moon reappears, I often go to the desert to pray for you. I pray, *Daughter, let these stars of night find bliss inside your mooning sky. Permit their inflamed dowry to enrich your dreams. An electric life exists just beyond the one you are living. Reach for it and howl. Awaken your precious soul.*

Becoming Woman

If you aspire to become a woman, it helps to make sure you know what a woman is. Otherwise you might become an elephant, a ball of angst, an anthill. Your intention has that much power. You may feel becoming an elephant is not such a bad deal. But what if you become an elephant uninformed of what it means to be an elephant? Now you are lost from your womanhood and your *elephanthood*.

Becoming what you set out to be, what you feel you are called to be, requires staying in close touch with the nature of that thing. This involves choosing teachers who themselves know what it means to be a woman. And those who remember what it meant to be a girl. The hardest part of growing up is adults who have forgotten the terror of growing up.

Question the womanhood blueprints offered you. Run those designs through your intuition. Discard some aspects, keep others. What you come up with is your own authentic womanhood. Approach women who are flowering in your eyes. Ask them to guide you. Ask for ceremonies, rituals, prayers. Invite other aspiring young women to join you in these gatherings. You are coming of age. Don't wait. Your age is coming.

Womaning

Have you been conditioned to be timid in the act of being a woman? *Being* is not a passive existence. Passivity is not life. Lively being is a choice, a freedom initiative, a permission to exist in ways that feel most like you. Some people don't want you to actively be a woman, whatever that means to you or them. This threatens them. Even your own family and friends can collectively wear down your active being of woman. Think of *womaning* as an investment in your wellness. You go running, swimming, walking, breathing, reading, writing, learning. Why not go *womaning*?

What does it mean to you to be *womaning*? Is it an angry, vengeful act or state? Or is it a beautiful thing? And what can you do with the harm done to you, now living in you as energy? You can transform it. To be an alchemist, all that is required is to access your energy, and care to use it. The more that has been done to you, the more energy you have available to do something with. This is how harm and trauma can be seeds in a beautiful life.

Harmony

Practice harmony, not conflict. Harmony is not meek subservience. It is bold communion. Harmony is the courageous sharing of your highest self, a chosen quarantine of your lower impulses to the back of the room, allowing goodness to do what goodness does. As you have learned to enjoy practicing many things in your life, you can learn to enjoy your harmony practice.

Do you find yourself saying people are getting on your nerves? Only you can get on your nerves. Get off your nerves. You own your reactions. Own them peacefully. At war with yourself and others, snow on your face feels like fire. Goodness you find becomes a grudge. Make light.

Rearrange the molecules of hurtfulness. Fashion healing crystals from tainted sand.

Learn to look for streams in you and streams in others that have a chance to flow together. Harmony matters because if you do not have it, you do not have wellness. You do not have music with the world. Or with yourself. Music is a habit. The outcome of playing in streams of rhythm, melody, and syncopation. Play there often.

Conflict does not exist for its own sake. It exists as a window into harmony, into peace. When the wind comes, lean toward Love. Always lean toward Love.

Social Illness

We fall into a world in which all we see is separation. Then, desperate, we spend life learning to see oneness again. One day, the hungry ghosts among humankind will realize the soul is real. And prejudice is only an idea. A foul imagination. Their chosen torment.

Oppression of womanhood is so pervasive, many of you accept it as righteous, rather than fight it and endure exhaustion. Oppression is an internal burial before it is an external one. You have profound dirt to remove from your lungs and your life just to reach up to the ground surface of being well. Take care, or your exhaustion and pain will open you to oppressing others in turn.

Your prejudices make you the monster. Tame them. You, of all people, should know the pain of receiving another's festering idea of you. The sting of being seen as inferior, unclean, unworthy, and unable. You are endowed with a sensitivity to erasure and degradation. Equipped to be on the front lines resisting the abuse of living things. Even if it sets you against your own Loved ones. Your tether to justice and honor is a potent rope. Take hold. Climb to courage, cleansing and healing any fungus growing in you.

Take the most tender care that you do not oppress any soul. Especially your own. Being dehumanized is a drowning. To resist is a furious revolt, a determined sweeping. Make your entire life a resistance movement against the sickness that says, *My kind is supreme*. A movement against the illness that has us bow before the supremacy lies of others. Your ultimate human duty is that you not demean your divinity. That you not sip inferiority, nor let its foulness stain your soul.

If your inner territory is to remain pristine, you must name your pollution. Or you cannot eradicate it. Stay in touch with our peculiar human poisons, that you may remain intimate with our triumphant human wellness. When a body has cancer, you don't plead to all the cells, *Why can't we all get along?* No, you kill the cancer. Supremacy is a cancer. You must name your cancer-poisons or they will kill you, daughter.

The moment you start telling yourself, *All men are...* or, *All women are...* you poison your soul, pollute your current and potential relationships, and keep beautiful souls far away from you. What healthy man wants to share his life with someone who generalizes, reduces, and dehumanizes men? What healthy, self Loving woman chooses to share her life with a person who demeans women the same way?

Anyone who wishes to taste your bitterness or who chooses to stay in it may have their own unwellness keeping them close to you. You perform a mutual blessing when you stay in your Loving spirit, which says, *Although we are inseparable from all things, every soul is divine and singular.* You have only known a small fraction of men or women. Your evidence for generalizing is weak. Your most fruitful assumption is the assumption that it is better for you not to assume.

We don't know how to talk about the truth, the root of our suffering, because we are a people who have avoided truth for centuries. All this suffering is our collective truth. It cannot be wished away. You cannot teach away hate and prejudice. It is not a matter of awareness or sensitivity. Love is the only detergent that cleans the soul. Love is painfully honest. It hurts before it heals.

When you choose to pretend to be blind to your prejudices, you are as a flame running through the forest setting everything on fire with your dishonesty.

Most of humanity will always be swimming for the center of the river, even though the river has no center. Those who believe they are the center, their profound soullessness will have them at the periphery, terrified by the truth. They will spend their lives propping up the illusion of their supremacy, though the curtain slips by the day. True humanity is a tide, inevitable, always rising.

When choosing whether to fill your heart with Love or hate, it is a matter of fit. Love, being the fluidity of spirit, fits better. Hate has jagged edges. It will perforate your heart and leak poison through your whole being. So, yes, your heart is shaped and designed for flow, for sacred rivers. For Love.

Do you wish to repeatedly tear up the flesh of your soul? I do not believe this. I believe you were born wanting peace and harmony with this life. Someone poured poison into the cup of your soul desire. Now you may be confused as to what you have a taste for. Taste pure Love. No additives. Nothing unnatural. Let your original appetite return.

True warriors don't make war. They make peace.
Especially inside the soul.

War is an illness, springs from illness, is the evolution of illness. War is not a wellness. We hurt the world because we do not recognize our *self* in it. You cannot plant poison and expect to eat paradise. Humankind is afraid to Love, timid and waiting. Yet we are ever ready to hate. Here, in the valley of this paradox, is where our work begins. And ends. Do not weaponize your heart. It has a higher calling. When hate roars, a frightened predator, release your Love's ocean. Drown the roar. This life is for Lovers. The only foreigner is one who does not Love.

Tolerance is not the issue. Oppression is. Say it. Say it, so you can feel it. Feel it, so you can face it. Do not live inside the cave of your fears. Step out into the brightness of your Love, which never stops calling for you. You hold a vital power. World change is born in a single heart. Your own.

Social World

Do you ever get the feeling that everybody except you is attending the greatest party ever? Such a lonely feeling. Search your story. It is tricking you. You aren't missing out. You're missing in. You miss your deepest self. The party is inside you. You're the host and the guest of honor. You've been invited. Don't stand outside looking through the window. Get the party started.

Make sure your social life is not death by social life. Put positivity and Love in. Take positivity and Love out. You have the right to leave the rest alone. If it doesn't help you grow, it needs to go.

What you share with your social world is no longer yours. It does not decay or fade away. It cannot forever be hidden. Your offering remains in that universe for anyone to use. Anytime. For any reason. Not just to embarrass you. To hurt you and those you Love and represent. Share goodness, and what you encounter will have more goodness in it. Honor yourself, your ancestors, and all who come after.

What you digest from the social world is in fact your diet. You can be meticulous about the food you eat, but if you aren't caring about your social diet, you can be just as filled with poison. Mental health largely reflects what you feed yourself. Images, words, sounds, and behavior are energy. They tattoo you more deeply than ink ever can. This energy flows into your soul energy and can overtake it. The filters that matter aren't photographic. Your intuition, instinct, experience, and intelligence filters make your life beautiful or full of harm.

Consider your soul line, your connection to the real and virtual worlds. Explore the nature of what gets shared through that network, the part of your life for which you ought to have the most powerful security. Attacks to your soul line are endless, insidious, and ever evolving. What is your antiviral program for your soul line?

Misery is contagious. The more you swim in a social river, the more you become the river. If the river is full of misery, sadness, negativity, and despair, this is the water you swallow. If you don't want to work hard at staying healthy, swim in healthy rivers.

Do not compare the depths of your life to the visible surface of another's. You cannot know their ocean. Do not abandon your own. Comparison can inspire you, though often it sickens your idea of yourself, like mirrors in a house of horrors.

Doing things for attention is like eating cotton candy. The response may feel good at first, but then the inevitable emptiness and sickness. The attention you seek from your insecurity holds no nutritional value. What you share soulfully returns to you as the food of life.

We cast out many pleas for social attention. All this *selfing* generates little self Love. Body-face focus can be nourishing or eroding, depending on how we use it. Clearly though, we are hurting in the soul. Maybe then, we can all benefit from more soul focus. Show us what your soul Loves in the world beyond your appearance.

The social world can inspire you and introduce you to your tribe. It can also be a death trap of comparison. Move through it with care. Care for yourself as you move through it. And always grant yourself freedom to step away and wash yourself clean. Daily. Loneliness can push you into harmful social desperation. Deeply feel the spirit of life in and all around you. Union this strong can cure your loneliness.

Seeds in any one of us are in every one of us. Ego says, *I am nothing like that person*. But that person is fruit of the same human tree that you are. Same soil, water, sun. One son is all sons. One daughter, all daughters. If you want to change the world, change your life.

Social attention can be an addictive drug. The initial high increasingly ends in a more painful bottoming out. You need stronger hits, more often. Those most drenched in social attention are often the loneliest, saddest, and most despairing. The fame you may want can erase your peace. Social attention will not improve how you feel about yourself. Only you can do that. When you pour yourself into the social world fueled by your compassion, caring, and curiosity, you can feed the world and yourself. Pour joy, creative spirit, discovery, healing, and wonder. Pour because Love compels you. Not anxiety, loneliness, or fear. Pour from your soul fire. You can light the lantern for our gathering of nations.

Shame

People use shame to control you, especially as a woman. Pay close attention to how shame grows in you, what sets it off, how you resolve it. Some deal with shame by growing more shameful, which is not dealing with it at all. You have been shamed since birth. Heal that, and you will be free. Gather your sisters and shed your shame.

Shame is how others take from you without consequence. Shame is how you bury yourself. How you keep your wounds bleeding. If you draw the arrow of your Love against the force of your shame, you can empower your Love to set fire to how you feel about yourself. You can burn down entire forests of unworthiness, until blue sky smiles on you again.

She found her voice when she lost her shame.

Two kinds of shame live in you. One comes from the world's judgment, or your mind's hoarding of false social ideas. This shame batters your soul. Another shame is produced by your mind as it recognizes your acts against the soul. This is an internal shame, a medicinal discomfort with harming yourself. This shame does not destroy. It offers itself as a dissonance for building your personal integrity. Living at peace with this shame empowers you to continuously correct yourself. To grow and improve. To feel the peace of harmony with your soul's sensitivity.

Some will shame you simply for being a woman. Or for supposedly *womanly things*, such as nursing your baby, even as they crave and consume the nakedness of women. Don't let their sick shame-fall rain on you. Hiding your nursing is not freedom. Neither is nakedness inherently freedom. Honoring your sacredness is. Be your own woman.

Shame is something trees know nothing about. Which is why they never stop growing. Imagine your life without shame. Vision it. Feel it. Find it. Your first breaths without shame may be unsettling. You may feel you are committing a crime. Continue forward. Soon, you will grow euphoric over the weightlessness of your life free of controlling shame. Your new language and ways will startle you even as they thrill you. Even as you inspire other women to shed their chains of shame.

Bullying

You may very well be your biggest bully. What has been done to you, you learn to do to yourself. This is how much we mirror each other. Whose voice is it inside you putting you down, mocking, scorning, doubting, and demeaning you? Are you sure this is the voice of others? Or are they the face you attach to the persistent voice that is now your own recording?

When you find yourself feeling humiliated and left out, you may be the culprit, the bully who has you backed into a corner. Confront your bully, even if it is you. Once you determine not to treat yourself this way any longer, you have begun a key journey into Loving yourself.

Bullies want to shame you. If you feel shame, you will shy away from telling anyone you have been bullied. Bullies don't want to be humiliated publicly. They want you to be humiliated in solitude. Find a way to share. Share your truth, that it may heal and not fester. Share creatively. Artistically. Not spitefully, this only deepens the wound. Share with your circles, your people, in spirit power.

Share in a spirit of Love for yourself. For those you care about who you don't want to experience the same harm. Share as an example, an inspiration for what to do with bullying. Share out loud. Share symbolically. Share with those you trust. If you share recklessly, you create more harm, inside and out. Honor your sharing with privacy.

Share with the kind of care any wound requires. Let the harm in you flow out of you. Let it pass through your Love on the way out, transforming into healing and light. Change the chemistry of it by giving it new birth.

Abuse

Abuse is a con artist. To live with the truth that you have been abused, your mind is instantly vulnerable to abuse justifying itself. Your mind generates rationales for the abuse. Acceptable reasons. Even as your mind grasps to hold onto truth, it wants to protect itself by explaining the abuse. This is how you begin to accommodate abuse. Understanding this is necessary for healing your mind back to truth.

How can you end up becoming abusive after you have suffered abuse? Once abuse is seeded into your inner story as a way of relating to people, this seed has the potential to sprout and grow, if watered enough. Even if you morally reject abusiveness, you can manifest abuse if you have watered its seeds now in you. These seeds are not just in some people. They exist in all of us.

Abusiveness is all around you, in countless forms. Seeds of abuse and abusiveness can enter your *soul soil* even indirectly. You do not have to have been directly abused. Even as I say this, I correct myself. All abuse is direct. If you see it, hear about it, imagine it, it is directly touching you. Caring for yourself is how to prevent the seeds from entering or sprouting in you.

If you struggle with treating yourself well, look at the relationships that raised you or that you were raised around. Look at the women in your life. How did they treat themselves and each other? Did any of those seeds, for better or for worse, blow over onto your ground and take seed in you?

You pick up abuse-nature like you pick up pollen outside in summer. Like fleas and ticks, it clings to you with a notorious skill, designed to go unnoticed, hitching a ride back home to the core of your identity. After being around abuse, scan yourself. Part your fine hair and look down into the pores of your skin. Ways of being have caught a ride with you.

If you abuse your children because you have been abused, you will have chosen to be an abusive spirit in the presence of your generations. You will have decided on a path that leaves suffering and dysfunction in the ones you Love most.

Are you a safe space? Not just for others. For you, dear. For you. You still have time. The seeds are in you. Break open your Love. We all require assurance, a delicacy best served by you to you. Becoming a safe space is one of the greatest gifts and legacies you can leave.

If those who raised you only knew how to be at war with themselves, you may have been raised to be at war with yourself. Go and find those who are at peace with themselves. They can teach you. They will want to. When you are at peace with your soul, you desire to spread that grace. You may have to teach yourself kindness. You can do it. You are a teacher. You have already learned much from yourself. Draft a better teacher evaluation.

Do not become what has been done to you. The temptation is strong. You do not have to become the degradation abuse leaves you feeling. You do not have to pass it on to others. You can take that ill spirit and overcome it with life spirit. Transform it into a passion that serves lives.

Even your tone of voice can seed the healing of a family's millennia of pain. Or it can open a wound more acute than human language can say. Medicine or weapon. You should have been raised by our tribe to know this power. Now, you are old enough to know.

You can forgive others and still remove yourself from their unwellness and hurtfulness. You can Love others and still stay out of their streams. You know the directions their waters are running, where they will sweep you. Stay in your river.

Daughters, every one of you has been violated in some manner. In some ways, daily. Life brims with trespasses. This truth does not lessen the terror or reverberation. Others, not even other women, cannot know your precise harm or what it means to you. Certain souls can relate enough to offer healing empathy and kinship.

I pray you will find your way to share your pain with others who can feel it. That you will testify. Each day, in your own way, testify. Expressing your truth exhumes your wholeness, keeps you afloat. Hold on to what you can. Grab for the reeds on the riverbank as you are swept along roughly and swiftly in the current of trauma.

Try not to violate yourself in return. Do not punish yourself when you most need gentleness. Acquaint yourself with the sickness inside violating souls, that it not breed a new sickness in you.

Go out to meadows alone and weep. Sit with the butterflies and blue skies and let them Love you. Go silent, and in your silence hear your healing song. We all have one. Hear yours. Open up your voice and shower the air with your meaning. And when you feel strong enough, start or join a revolution against the abuse of womanhood. You can assert yourself and not hurt yourself. You can demand honor and still hold your heart like a feather in a gentle sea.

Your experience cannot be removed. But it is full of meaning. Only you can harvest this. And why would you? Because meaning picked and plucked and shucked and cleaned becomes a meal that brings you back, that brings us back as we dine with you. Back to the truth of sickness and the truth of wellness and the essence of our duty.

We need these feedings, as many as we can get. We are all starving and we need your story, daughter. The story of the meaning you draw from the well water of your journey. Please, enlighten us. What does it mean to be you? In seeing through your window, we see something more of ourselves. Every violation needs acts of Love to rebalance the world. The Love acts that spill from your heart have a special power to them. Please, feed us.

Pay at least as much attention to your forms of violence against yourself as you do to the violence of others against you. Gentleness and tenderness are not the opposite of violence. They are not related. Gentle and tender treatment is how Love behaves. Violence grows from hurt and suffering, which are not the opposite of Love, but instead are greatly in need of Love.

Doubting yourself is a violence. Not giving yourself permission for anything soulful can be a violence of oppression. It is violent of you to practice chronic anxiety. The damage this does to your body, brain, and being is real and lasting.

You always have an opportunity to learn about the roots of your self harm. When you harm yourself, you are harming much more than yourself. In this way, self harm is a misnomer. You either harm the whole world, or you heal it. Everything else is delusion.

Children see how we harm ourselves. This causes them great pain even as they stow away the lesson plan of self harm in their cellular garden. Use this as motivation to heal. Don't beat yourself up. Forgiving yourself is a root of no longer hurting yourself. You say you do not know how to begin Loving yourself. Make an agreement with your soul: *No more beating myself up. No more putting myself down. Love talk only. Forever.*

A girl approaching womanhood was filled with a vision of her life ahead. In her vision, she stopped beating herself up and putting herself down. Instead, she lifted herself up. Her soul flowered. She Loved her new altitude.

Gossip

The truth is, we are terrified. Gossip is a security blanket we wrap around us. The blanket is infested with self loathing and the lice of malice. What we feel protects us leaves us more terrified, seeking more gossip. This does not end until you make a brave choice to burn the blanket and learn a true way of securing yourself.

Sometimes gossip is protective of your tribe. In this way, it can be a primal impulse. Often though, it is an ugly flare from fear's mouth. You can pollute and destroy your world and your soul with gossip. You can destroy even your Love for yourself. Love does not grow in ugliness. It needs a different kind of soil. If you must gossip, spread word of someone's goodness. Be an earth maker, fertile ground for beauty.

Predators and Prey

We are not innately born as predator or as prey. And yes, anyone can be predator or prey. But a deeper cultural truth demands our reckoning:

With Love I say, although many men are not predators, we do culturally train boys to become that fate. From birth they are marinated in a world saying to them, *Take. Take what you want. Use physical force. Intimidate. Threaten. Especially use girls and women. Turn your natural affinity for them into ferocious resentment. Women are your jewelry, your instrument for gain, your accompaniment, your repository for wrongly used fear and desire.*

Though many escape, we train girls to be prey. We say to them, *Seek out a home in others. Do not be a home to yourself. Be dependent. Offer yourself for what you need. Offer your body, but more than that, offer the sacrifice of your selfhood, of your wholeness. Give away yourself so you may have the things we train you to want. Not what your soul wants. Identify yourself not with soul power and freedom but with slavery, with being owned. Crouch. Shrink. Be quiet. Use your voice upon penalty of death. Death by rejections and criticism and ridicule.*

The predator in us, women and men both, says to girls, *Need things. Things for false acceptance and superficial belonging. Go look for your master, your savior, your knight. Turn out your own light. Go looking blindly, desperately, as though you are nothing unless you wed yourself to a man. And not even a man who would honor you. A man who is not a man. A man who cannot know you because he does not know himself. A man who uses you. Yes, be used. Be used by family, friends, colleagues. Be used by our fear of you. Whatever you do, do not dare Love yourself. Do not take up space, breathe, or stand up. Back up, move to the side, forget yourself. Remember your duties. Duties we ascribe. You are property. You are not proper unless you act and think and feel as property.*

With all the Love in me, I pray you reject this proposal. It has no authority. It is a fraudulent reality propped up for centuries by frightened souls, male and female and otherwise. Daughters, kill the slave in you. Scratch, and weep, and laugh, and fight your way to freedom. Stay far away from the slave and the master. Learn a way of being that rejects ownership. Prey moves in a tense fright through its life, a doomed rabbit. It waits for cover, acts to avoid encounters and conflicts. Seeks out shelter and shadows to the neglect of openness and light.

In any kind of relationship a person can groom you to be whatever they want to use you for. Your life depends on recognizing sincere caring. When you find yourself in the seductive hands of a predator, your vulnerabilities are being caressed. Understand that from the very beginning you are being prepared, tenderized, trained.

Look for the subtle signs of grooming. Their language says much. Do they tell you they will be the father, mother, Lover, friend you never had? That they understand you better than anyone can? That they can provide for you and you will never have to work or worry again? Do they doubt and discourage your gifts and skills and passions? Do they separate you from your friends and family, especially the ones who have healthy lives and instinct? Do they break you down, then build you up? Beat you up and then calm you down? Slather you with gifts and compliments when they want something from you, then threaten to take those gifts away?

Predators share a common language. They are gifted at appearing to be your personal savior. They are the knight in shining armor, except beneath the armor a danger lurks. They are the mother of your dreams, the father, girlfriend, boyfriend, soulmate you prayed for. They have a way of sensing your dreams, of playing your fears, of leading you in your sleepwalk over a cliff before you know it. You will not want to betray them, even as you betray your soul. You will want a life with them, even as you give away your life.

Predators sense vulnerability, needfulness, insecurity, and passivity. If you have these qualities, surround them with people who are the opposite. It keeps predators away, allowing you to grow your power.

You can recognize a predator if you learn to recognize the pain and yearning in you. Predators will be the ones who feel good to the needful part of you, even as their energy stokes a vivid fear. You will want them to be your shelter, your protection, your confidant. Confide in your instinct. Each time you do, your instinct grows. Confide in your intuition, in your intelligence, in those who tell you the truth even as it stings. Confide not in the comfort of denial but in the creation of your life. Express your struggle in ways that make you safer, not more exposed. Endure the thorn. Achieve the rose.

Pray that you Love yourself. You are not prey.
Pray. Love yourself with a wild fire.

Daughter, you need not blush at predatory compliments. You are not prey. You are priceless. I pray you will not consume predatory compliments as your daily nutrition, and that you will look into the mirror of sacred Love for the reflection of your truest, divine worth. When someone calls you *beautiful*, this does not grant that person the right to possess or violate you.

Appreciate what your soul feels are pure compliments. Use them thoughtfully as windows for seeing and embracing your own glory. Just don't grow addicted. Even healthy compliments do not determine you, and can bury you in dependency, a hard hole to escape.

It is time for all souls to shed the shackles of superficial beauty and birth a spiritual era that honors a living thing. Predatory compliments are cover for the truth that someone so much wants to eat your flesh that they are more than happy to also eat your soul.

Many people use the word *beautiful* as a lure with you. As though the more they say *beautiful* to you, the more you will open to them, give them what they want. They hope to lure you in with each casting of that spell, that bait-word, *beautiful*. You are not a fish. Not a tin can to be pried open with verbal devices. You are not for sale. And if your hunger for affection or belonging is not misplaced, no predator may easily have you.

Not needing attention
or a compliment is self Love too.

When does the word *beautiful* and its versions become a girl's drug addiction? Who are the dealers? We must reckon with this. It is killing our spirit. It is time to gather our healers and smoke out the truth.

You have predators at work. In school. Wherever you are, they are. This is the nature of predators. Some look like you. Still, they want things from you and will consume you to get it. If you tell yourself all the things your heart desires to hear, all the words, you will not be as hungry. You will not go looking into dangerous dens and caves for what is freely yours in the openness of your heart.

Predators suffer greatly. They exist in a cage of torment and fear, slave to their malice and addiction to harm. Put them out of their misery. Come together with others who care enough to end predation. Learn how not to be prey. You are not responsible for predators. Your duty is freedom. Hold predators accountable. Shaming is not the point. Enlightening your tribe to danger is the point. Love yourself richly. Unlearn guilt. Testify and witness and seek shelter with your sisters and others who have been preyed upon. You can be free.

A Life of Healing

One of the most powerful points in your healing journey is when you realize this awesome truth: *I do not have to suffer. I can choose.* When this dawning first happens, entire flocks of anxiety and fear fly away from you, and a lightness enters, an astounding birth of peace.

Life is a circle of pollution and purification. You are always being polluted. You must always purify: breath, thoughts, speech, heart, soul, body, memories, desires, imagination. Learn from the souls who make purity their life. When they pass by, a sweetness mists the air and living things open.

To say, *I don't need healing*, is to be blind to the natural circle of life happening in you and all around you. Harm is a river, and you are in its purposeful current. In life, harm is continuous. Always be healing. All day, every day, you are being weathered by life. Cleanse your soul daily.

> *Daily she told the little girl inside her,*
> You are safe now.
> *The girl became a woman.*

The inner girls and boys in others are tugging at your inner girl's arm on the playground of life, saying, *Come on. Be like us. Don't you want to be one of us?* You don't have to let her be one of them. Those inner children are often stuck in the moments of their development when hailstorms of trauma fell on them. They aren't *growing anywhere.* Your inner child may want to run with the others. But do you want her growth to be paralyzed by their influence? You can keep her growing. With enough nurturing, she can catch up to you, reach where you are on your growth journey. When this happens, what a peace inside. Harmony. Synchronicity in your soul.

You believe your soul is calling you Healer.
Listen closely. It is saying, Heal her.
Heal the little girl inside.

She is ready. Care for the girl in you. If you learn to speak with her in a voice and tone that soothes her, she calms down. You calm down. She is a ripple. You are the shore. Her emotional states and thoughts precede yours. Result from yours. She is you and you are her. She looks up to you. This gives you a certain power and duty. You can show her healthful ways, teach her peace.

Your truth and openness bless you, bless us all. You are to be admired, not for your journey, but for your *truthing* of it, for your choice to alchemize your life into sacredness. Sacredness has a breath. That breath is truth. Healers can have the deepest wounds. But they Love them well.

So many of your interpretations of life cause your heart and soul to constrict. Many other translations cause them to open. This is another way of looking at healing: The exercise you do to stay dilated. Only then can goodness get through.

Healing is not polite. It speaks truth. It gathers truth. It wades and wallows in truth. It behaves, remembers, and feels truthfully. These traits deeply disturb denial and deceit. Truth-traits shake up the world, which senses it is dying, not realizing it is also being born. What we feel now is the tearing away of our layers of docile comfort, truth serrating unwellness from wellness. We are in a healing time, raw and courageous, relearning what it means to be all the way alive.

You will have times when you fold yourself into an origami of a thousand cranes and take flight on the billowing of your dreams. And you will have times when you bloom like a quiet flower by a soft stream and weep such a precious song. Have faith, now. It won't be long.

If you wish to experience yourself in a way that heals and builds you, participate in the healing and building of others like you. You will learn things along the way. Old ways and ancient memories will come alive in the ashes piled high by self centeredness. You will have the spark and smoke for new fire.

The way a river lives with its water,
live with what heals you.

You wash your hands faithfully throughout your day. You believe in the power of soap, water, and friction. You believe that without this washing, you would become sickened and sicken others. Imagine if we faithfully washed our spirits clean throughout each day? If we believed in the power of attention, Love, and intent? If you wash your spirit clean as you go, you can remain well and help keep others well. Spiritual hygiene is a gift.

If you have tender places inside, tend them. Your pain is a kindness that speaks to you in phrases like, *I could use your attention right now*. We spend our life searching for healers, but we are the medicine. The miracle of your design is that you are self repairing. First though, you must realize your true nature. You aren't just capable of healing, you are Healing itself. Spread your Love potion the way we spread angst and fear, and you are salve to the world's woundedness. You aren't here to be unwell. You exist to carry wellness to every soul. Your new name is *Sacred Medicine*. Go live up to your true name.

The girls and women in your life may Love you more than their hearts can hold. This alone does not prevent them from conditioning you as they have been conditioned. They, through the seeds they carry, might be your nearest slaves. Boys and men don't always pose the greatest danger to your freedom, to your safety and fulfillment. On every plantation, slave controls and conditions slave, more than slave master ever can.

Pay attention to who is encouraging you to sell your soul, prostitute your sacredness, mute your voice, stay in your place, despise maleness, objectify your femaleness, or regard relationship as a battleground. Who is passing on their wounds to you? Are you graciously accepting the anti-gift? Whose viral unwellness is embedding in you?

Because you are a sacred vessel, you must keep your inside clean and supple for what comes through. And what comes through? Oceans. Rivers. Skies. Ancestors with baskets of prayers, blood, and tears. Love's enormity. Hope weavings. Things on fire. Waking mountains. Panthers of the night. Seeds with cracked shells. Pollen. Nectar. Fancy dancers. Medicine in jars of soul. Warriors. Vision seers. Healers. Wild horses. Sunrises. Breaths of universe. It is not easy being a sacred vessel. It is an honor. A sovereign duty. Everything.

Life is a tide that can sweep you out into the deep water far from the shore of your truth. Self Love and self care are the strokes you take to swim back home. Breathe beautifully. Release everything. Bathe in your soul's natural affirmation. Stay in sight of your shore. Keep returning to you. Peace promises to be waiting.

The first healing act is when you stop partitioning your heart and soul, and choose to let Love run rampant through life's totality. Healing is not a territory or a hoarding. It is a boundless testimony. What is poured is never for one soul, but for all souls, if only every soul opens to the offering. An offering that comes not from you, but through you, when you choose to be its vessel.

Some people have negative ideas about healing. They associate it with unwellness or weakness or even guilt. They scorn the idea of healing or anyone who needs it.

They need it. Healing is in you as a matter of being alive. Your need to heal is as constant as your need to breathe. You are a planetary body forever bombarded by foreign objects and extreme energies. You are cratered and pocked like the moon. Internally and externally, you are a ribbon flexing and wavering as conditions change. You harbor obstructed rivers and swollen tissue. Tenderness.

Trauma from power-abuse and oppression is the massive nature of our human condition. Nurturing souls is not a competition, a favoring, but rather a devotion to pouring Love unconditionally. One group's suffering does not preclude the truth of another group's suffering.

Superficial self care on top of neglected self Love can conceal unwellness and delay true healing. If you dig deeper and reach the roots of your suffering, if you touch those tendrils with care, your ache becomes a poem. True self care is an innate poem sung by the breath of self Love. Self Love is a fire you tend. Self care is the heat that naturally arises to keep your soul supple and warm.

When you say you are a healer, you do not claim to heal others. Healing is the realm of the personal. You can hug people, but until they hug themselves, no true embrace is born inside. You can Love others, but until they blatantly Love themselves, your Love cannot bloom in them. You can hope for the best for others, but until they kindle hope in their own soul, the light of becoming is no more than a faint trembling on a far horizon. When someone truly travels the healing way, a sermon occurs between suffering and promise. A scripture profound and indecipherable to all but the one who dares so extraordinary an odyssey.

Often, your first step is to believe you can heal, to believe you can support others in their healing. Deep down inside, wellness is an identity. Your power lives in the names you call yourself. When you care for you, you care for every soul in your life. Grow your garden. Nurture your garden. Everybody feasts from your harvest.

If you are going to hold up, repair, mend other lives, nurture your own. Passionately. Immensely. Our kind hosts a burning that never leaves us. Tender as dew, devoted as sunrise, it goes on. A tendril of incense smoke, curling and quaint. Vast blazing tide. Where hurt is, we are. We weave at dawn, in the cool silence. Our bright tears form Love's offering. Corn pollen stains our fingers. Out in the tall crops, our backs ache a sincere communion. Noon's fire finds us at the river, reclaiming hymns for a soul revival. We carry medicine water the long way home.

How to be an oasis for others: Breathe deeply. Speak gently. Smile easily. Let all your light out to play. Slow down. Be peace. Exude peace. Tame your anxiety. Listen with your heart. Be all the way with them. Don't rush them. Invite their truth. Don't judge. Bathe them in your essential oils of Love and compassion. Massage them with mercy. Be deeply grateful. And, of course, to be a spa for others, we must first learn to be a spa for ourselves: same recipe. Over and over again.

The deepest trauma in you is not a curse. It is a miraculous reflection pond. If you kneel and face it with your whole heart, you will see yourself as you are meant to be. If you feel sick in your soul, tune your soul to Love's frequency. Love is the answer. Suffering is the riddle. Love will heal you. But first you must drown in it. What you were must die, that you may live.

Good news. You have the innate ability to heal your soul. Has your body healed? Your heart? You are a healer. Each day, you repair your cells, mind, memories, attitude, heart, relations, spirit, feelings, and dreams. If you don't believe you are a healer, you have not been witnessing your own life.

Make medicine with your pain.
Be that kind of warrior.

Recognize that when you choose new ways, and those new ways heal old pain, that too is Loving yourself. With your every touch, gaze, thought, feeling, word, imagination, make medicine. Anything can grow if it is well-Loved. Even your most shattered you. The Love within you is medicinal, with no harmful side effects. Please, self medicate. Self Love is an immune system. It kills the virus of self harm.

Heal just a grain of you, and the whole world inherits your many blessings. This world is very tender now because it is giving birth to a whole new world. Birth feels like this. To heal the world, begin inside. This is how you touch the suffering tide. Work the root. Your soul determines us.

We are weary now. We don't care for our wounds. We misunderstand what true caring is. Our wounds overtake us. Unwell in the soul, we devour each other, the worst eating disorder of all. The way we live shears away light from our aura like old paint. Beneath the layers, clandestine joy waits for our revival. That weak trickle moving through your weariness is Love. Make it a river. Be renewed. Plant your soul in the rich earth of sacred Love. Reforest beauty.

You do not need artificial things to renew your soul. Spend an entire day in poetry, stories, dance, and song, listening to the song of Creation. You will be new. When you behave in your intrinsic ways, unpolluted and purified, you are medicine. Health is a continuous releasing, continuous birthing. Sit by a river or a tree and see how health behaves. Make medicine with today. It has all the ingredients for healing.

The Loving touch of your deep attention goes a long way. You may feel more comfortable offering it to others. When your tender wounds receive it, you become your own best masseuse. Simplify your healing. Kiss your tenderness. Speak only words that heal.

Healing is not a competition.

You do not have to be hard, a prison against the soul. Your softness can be everything. Especially freedom. Even the slightest tenderness requires healing. Do it your way. Take your time. Do not compare your healing to that of others. You do not know their journey. Affirm yourself as you go. And know that you will rise. For your soul is kin to sun, born of skies. Your healing is a great wind. A great, wild water. A chosen movement home.

Release and Surrender

We seek shelter in perceived permanence. Life though is a continuous letting go. If you do not surrender to this river, if you fight this current, you suffer. Holding onto things is like trying to control a wild hawk in your hands. It won't stop fighting you. In the end, you kill the hawk or finally let it go. Either way, your hands are left shredded and bleeding. The hawk did not do that to you. You did it to yourself. A great wisdom exists in letting go.

You know the voice of your soul. It is the feeling of resistance or surrender you experience in every moment. You are either resisting or surrendering to your soul. Give yourself to what stirs your soul. If you surrender, your seeds of promise will grow into an awesome paradise. Habit is a chosen surrender. Surrender to things that serve your life. A beautiful life is not built. It is released. Freedom. Loving yourself means letting go.

In a world of frightened clutching and grasping, you could be a totem pole for peace, a place where tranquility gathers. What a tree feels as leaves come and go, and how it is with birds on its branches, be like that with change. Sunrise is a good reminder. Darkness serves its purpose. Then it becomes light. Pay attention to the way moonlight communicates, how an icicle lets go of its water. Teachers are everywhere. Look out at life. Your true nature is happening.

You cannot make others activate their true power. They must want it enough. It is worth your patience as they move in that direction. Once they light that sacred ember, they become wildfire. The world is made anew.

Be frugal with blame. It tends to instantly destroy inner peace and inner power, all at once. Burn away all the blame in your heart, blame for you, for anyone, anything. What remains will be the peace you seek, a freedom that lives as truth.

Trauma and fear cause you to try too hard. At everything. Trying too hard has a scent and energy to it. No one likes to feel that pressurized atmosphere coming from you. *Not trying* can be a great freedom, a complete peace as you fall at last into the sweet sufficiency of being. Look how many ways life is Loving you. Accept the flowers.

Tenderness

Because you feel, you feel worldly pain in you. This is the nature of a feeling thing. A feather adrift high in the sky is felt as a ripple deep in the water. You are that water. If you can feel an ant approaching an aphid, and the anxiety between them, you are a sensitive creature. This is why you are here.

*A butterfly lands on a thousand flowers
and never leaves a single bruise.
Touch your heart like that.*

Do you feel deeply? Then that must be what the world needs from you. Don't shallow water yourself. Plunge. Not into despair. Into the sweet communion of what lives and Loves and learns and laughs and lights in the deeper waters of the soul. Whale song is a glorious chorus. Join them in the ecstasy. Give thanks for feeling life this vibrantly. Your sensitivity is called *being deeply alive*. You gather meaning through feeling. Soul wealth is measured this way. Feel deeply. Touch your wealth. If you feel part of the way, you heal part of the way. Feel all the way. You will be all the way alive.

The tender places in your heart are soil for your seeds of healing. Garden there. Touch, address your tenderness. That's all it ever wanted. Hardness breaks. Softness surrenders to its seasons. Love not harder, but softer. Be soil for beautiful things. A soft heart lets healing seeds bed down. And peace come to sprout.

Your body is a lake holding all your energy. A fine-tuned water. Your immune system cannot bear chronic imbalance, ripples in the water. Disease in your body is a warning flower. You cannot afford to harbor negative, violent ripples. Release them. Heal your water.

Softness. Not because you are a woman. But because it is the nature of living things. And you are a living thing. Seeds. Soil. Surrender. Softness is a ceremony. A true Loving of you. Your soul is a soil. Countless seeds and flowers. Work your soil. Deep feeling souls must be gardened. Your heart is a tender land. Sing to it like a Lover. You can never have too much tenderness.

The way a leaf lands on lake water. Feel like that. You can feel gently and still send ripples all the way to your shore.

You can be gentle with your heart through anything. Learn how to hold your heart. It is a vital art. Start.

Touch today gently. With caring and Love. It will touch you back. Easy does it. Gentleness is a power and a medicine all at once. More gentleness. Start with you. Gentleness is a gentle nest for tenderness. Invest in the suppleness of your innerness.

Snow does not navigate sky on its way down to earth. It surrenders. Its reward is a softness in life, a silence of being that could be called the sound of glory.

She slept peacefully knowing that today
she had been kind to herself. And true.

What grapes do on the vine is a patient art. What sun does inside grapes is a miracle. You can be grape, vine, sun, all the splendor of that sacred dance. You can gift yourself right now with something Loving and gentle: patience. Day by day. Building healthy ways is a gradual art. A patient kind of Love work.

––––––

The women gaze at an elder woman, admiring. She swims in the milk of moon. Bathes in the honey of sun. Floats in the sea of her meditated soul. Her life is a river of jubilation and serenity, all because she gardens her thoughts. Tenderly.

Purpose of Your Pain

Everything changes the day you realize your pain is a seed for your power. That if you water and care for it, it can become energy for your beautiful life. On that day, you taste the first salt of an extraordinary sea.

As thirst leads you to water, suffering is one way your soul moves you closer to what it needs. When you hurt, you are being pointed in a clear direction. All you have to do is go there.

She took the pain and Loved it
into a whole new color.

Pain can tear you to *peaces*. Peace of humility, surrender, brokenness. Peace of healing, growing, truth. Peace of remembering yourself. Peace of determination. Peace of insight, hindsight, foresight. Peace of awakening.

It is not true that we descend from human beings. We are the offspring of joy and pain. What came before us spilled into us. What comes after tugs forever on our souls. We are a medley river. Irretrievably immersed.

Your pain is not your pain. It belongs to the river of generations. To be used in each era in their own ways. Used to build things. To plunder suffering for its fruit. To enter deeper yet into the mystery and cup the water of knowing in your palms. Try not to carry your pain as though it is yours alone. This is an unnecessary burden. In your mind, in a spirit of kindness, give your pain away, bread to the masses. Give it away as tender lessons. It is yeast for your compassion. Let it rise.

Your anger is not your anger. It is a hurt passed down for generations, latent and waiting in your heart. Anger creates amnesia. You forget your true nature. Love in you is obstructed in a flash. A stroke occurs. When the panic of rage or hurt sets in, it is as though the soul is a helpless lamb confronted by a ferocious lion. Remind yourself: *Only my mind is telling me this story. I can always tell myself that story time is over.*

Do not let your pain become a harmful surge protector. Closing your heart is an understandable reaction to the inward surge of hurt. But it also blocks the heart from its natural outward surging into Love.

Polish your pain until it shines like the midday sun, blessing everything and everyone. That's the thing to do with a heartbeat come undone. Don't wrestle your pain. It is a boa constrictor. It will win. Love talk your pain. Love talk works better. Get it drunk on that ancient wine.

Pain is a curtain. On the other side is the rest of your life. You don't want out of this world. You want out of your pain. Stay in the world, and you can climb out of your pain. How do we know this? Healing is our human story. Every soul has said, *No one hurts as badly as I do now. This pain is impossible.* The world is full of those very same souls. They have endured the impossible. Now they know the power of possibility. Survive great pain, and you learn to laugh at fear. You learn to live.

How do you speak to your suffering? Do you treat it as a tyrant, saying, *Beat me some more?* Treat it as a Loved one, saying, *I feel you. I am with you. We are going to take care of each other. You teach me. I will heal you. Together, we will go forward and soon we will have stories of this day. We will laugh and cry and remember.*

Pain carves you. You can become a hopeless abyss. Or you can become a grand canyon. The grooves in you of healed pain can hold Love the way earth grooves hold water. Your pain carvings do not leave you less. Healed and healing, they leave you more.

Sometimes, it hurts. Use those moments. Pain holds a million teachers. Enroll with every one of them. Graduate. Repeatedly, you choose to be a slave. Each time, pain. This is the soul's way of teaching you to be free. After each storm, gather hope. Notice what remains. Notice your heart. A lantern on the silent water. Still glowing.

River stones don't complain about the water polishing them. Pain is a mystic water. It makes no sense. Until it does. If you are alive, hope lives. Like a spring blossom in the gentle breeze, Love is lifting you. Pain, like an old, brittle seed in a patient bed of earth, one day too will crack. What tender glory then to seek the sun.

She wrote a Love letter to herself every day.
That's how she got through it.

Self Love is a daily art. Cherish your craft. Hold your heart like a Lover. It needs you more than you know. Touch your pain with all the Love in you. It will surrender one day. Aching is a beautiful seed, and means more than does the frequency of rituals. Ache it into the world. Butter it with Love. Braise it with Love. Hold it with the awe of a Lover. You are one. You know you are.

She walked through fire.
That's why she's so well done.

Some are soulfully seasoned by the splendor of the sojourn and its serendipitous seasons of surrender. Use your heartaches. They are spiritual currency. Seeds waiting for you to grow them into Love, light, laughter.

Grieving

Grief is a tidal creature. It lifts, surges, swells, recedes. We think we can time its rhythms, but its rhythm is beyond our understanding. At times it feels heavy, an unbearable crushing. We move slowly through a dark tunnel, holding our breath until we reach the other side. But the other side taunts us, keeps moving farther back, it seems. We are running out of breath. Just before we lose consciousness, a dim light flutters across our skin. We may not even be aware that the pain has lightened for a moment. We can breathe. *Hope. Maybe I can make it through this.*

Lost in the tender touch of those who Love us, lost in their being lost with us, something happens. Time can explain this better, though it never does. Instead, time tosses us into a strange dream no words can say. This dream is a time machine. It rearranges us forever. One day. One morning. One moment, we wake. From the dream. Still, we teeter on its edges. Pain's tide has pulled away, back into itself. Not forever. Far enough and for long enough that we can walk the sand. And see and touch and hold and caress the bright, polished stones of sweet memory now revealed.

Now we can hold the Love water we have for the soul we want back in human form, and not leak. Now we can bear the barnacles of pain carving our Love. Now we are able to live barefoot on the fine silted coral of this change, and bleed bravely, and have blood's sorrow swim with a kind of grace out into the salt of a gentler sea.

Daughter, we have taught you that grieving is a negative thing. An imposition and inconvenience we all wish you would get over with soon and move on, letting us move on. We have harmed you gravely through this teaching. Your grief is an expression of what a thing means to you. Its intensity reflects the intensity of your Love and attachment. The sun's heat is intense because it comes from the sun. Your grief is intense because it is offspring of your Love and attachment.

You do not have to judge your attachments as being good or bad to take care of how you are affected by them. Letting go is hard because you held tightly in the first place. But was your grip a perfect reflection of your Love, or was it also a measure of your fears, insecurities, and desires? Your grief is an opportunity to honor and celebrate all of this, even as it pulls away from you.

Cleaving hurts. It also reveals the deeper flesh and bone. Your grief reveals to you the true and false meaning of a relationship. It reveals you. If you grieve completely, your ideas of you are cleaved away, more than your relationship can ever be. You are born again. What you find then can be what you care to change or cherish more deeply than ever.

Cultures have rules for grieving. Follow them if they serve you. Let them go if they impede your authentic grief. This is your grief journey: figuring out what works for you, and learning to deal with other people's expectations about your grief. If you put a clock on your grief, your grief will clock you. If you try to bury your grief, your grief will bury you. If you let your grief be free, your grief can free you. Your grief is a living thing. Not an idea or a social schedule. It breathes, feels, has moods, and needs. You know how to care for living things. You have been doing it all your life. Be available for your grief. And when remembering, make sure to remember in a way that heals and makes even your most tender heart smile.

Joyfulness

If you are joyful at night, take joy to sleep with you. If you are joyful in the morning, take it to work with you. Take joy into your Love making, your laughter, your tears. Bring joy along for your whole life. Joy is a swelling of the heart, flushing of the soul. It softens your hardness for your river song of moments. It's how you get through the tight spaces like water doing yoga poses. It's the dew on your passion roses. Make joy offerings with every breath.

The joy you want is doing a miraculous thing. It has been waiting patiently inside you all your life. It believes in you. When you are ready, it will bloom.

Breathe with your life, not just your lungs. Smile with your Love, not just your face. If you do a thing joyfully, it means your heart and soul are open. More life rushes in.

Be a better banker. Bring in more life than you are giving away. In fleeting moments with others, open into joy. Not just your joy. Joy itself. Your moments will be a riper fruit.

If joy is a drought in your heart, create rain. Summon a mad preacher raised in a carnival to keep you properly aloft in delirium's sky. Don't keep looking for almond peddlers. Grow an almond tree. Watching a squirrel is fun. Climbing a tree is more fun. You don't always have to rhyme this life. Rhythm is the thing.

Happiness is a happening. That's why it's called happiness. It is an act. A vibrant, intentional unfolding. Like an orchid petal from its tuck. Or your heart dilating into joy. A conspiracy of sunlight. A choice to remember beauty, to harvest its bounty. Happiness is not a state. Not an accidental outcome. It is a happening. Decipher your soul and story. Make happiness happen.

If you are going to feed yourself, hydrate yourself, and rest yourself, why not bliss yourself. To stay in the energy of bliss, apply bliss. Intentionally breathe, think, feel, remember, and cherish bliss. Blissfulness does not occur by accident. It is an accumulation. Bliss you.

It is good not to interrupt your own joy. Let it have you as long as it wants you. Joy cannot be purchased. It is a living thing. It must be gardened. Watered. Whispered to. Open your soul window. Feel the inner breeze. Don't stop crying joy. Be the loudest one laughing. Laughter is not just medicine. It is a smoke signal that says to hope, *Come stay with me.* Congratulate your joy. It has worked remarkably hard to stay wild in you.

Fall in Love with your own joy and movement. You are not an inert object. You are a phenomenon of freedom. In the bright decadence of your joy, your soul prays you will remember this feeling and bring it with you everywhere you go. For a beautiful life, look upon others as you do all natural wonders. Don't tighten and close. Open and awe. Be a soft meadow. Beauty will arrive.

Creative Life

Soul is a profound ocean. What rises from it is mist for you to release. If you do not, this mist grows heavy, hardens, then falls back into your ocean. Your soul-ocean grows burdened this way. When you create, you are honoring your soul, and all the rivers running through you.

Creativity, the ultimate dilation we call Love, is a sacred birthing. And in birthing, you are born. Birthing changes you. It is a sacrificing of selfhood into the hungry mouth of the collective. You are at your most vulnerable and powerful as you birth. Being wide open is a state of potential. Things enter and leave you. Spiritual offspring are loosed upon the world. Creativity, which is Love, is a divine fertilizer, imbuing life with life. Choose to create. And be gentle. As you birth, you are being born.

Through creative expression you can shed a thousand skins and bare your soul to its own birthing. You can taste honey rain in the desert and make Love with all that is, on a mountaintop. You can drown your identities in a water drop and forge new fire with each kindling word. If you let your soul go swimming in black lakes of ink, in curling rapids and fonts, something beyond reason happens. Ecstasy.

In your lifetime you will find things
that make your heart leap.
Make that your art.

Creativity is your soul's way of rejoicing. And rebelling. And saving itself. Creativity is fertility, the birthing of things. Life is a ceaseless dying. Without continuous birthing, you and your life reach a point of desolation.

When was the last time you danced to the music of your own soul? It is time again. It is always time again.

They told her to be tame and timid.
So she danced until wild things joined her.

To say, *I am not creative*, is to miss seeing yourself. To be alive is to be creative. Your cells are all dancing, singing, creating. It is not a matter of whether you are creating, but how wonderfully. *Wonder. Fully.* To create is to breathe. Are you breathing apologetically? Or are you breathing as though you are entirely made of air? No boundaries or capacities. Just be with everything.

Everything is dancing, singing, praising. Can you feel this sweet music called life? Throw away your old clothes that muffle all glory, all expression. Be naked in this miracle. Have no shame. Touch your life like a potter's hands make Love to wet clay on the wheel. Don't just create. Give birth. Be birthed. Stain yourself in earth and water. Feel this turning. Weep your life away.

If a song doesn't sing, it suffers. You are a song. If a dancer doesn't dance. If a blossom doesn't bloom. Resisting what you are is a root of much suffering. Being what you are is life.

You are a poem. A song. A dance. A ceremony. What I mean by this does not matter as much as what you mean by this. Stay in touch with your words, your rhythm, melody, harmony, and rituals. Gather your wild meanings and feast on them. Clean and prepare them well. Staying well is a life of gathering, and of releasing. If you aren't feeling like a song, maybe your music has been muted. Clear away foreign, false noise and it will return. If you do not feel like a dance, how has your movement been stilted? Go to the origin of your paralysis and gently wake your soul.

You have poetry in your bones. Suck the marrow. If you write a single word and your heart lives in it, you have written a masterpiece. As you plant your olive and lemon groves, your almond and fig trees, also plant your poet-trees, trees bearing fruit whose juices stain the soul.

Your soul at peace is poetry. If you hear the right poem in the right moment, with the right light, the right heart, you can be reborn. You are poetry. Recite yourself. How you treat yourself and others is your most authentic poetry. Recite all the Love poems this life brings you. Use your softest voice. Worship this way.

Life has four elements or teachers, four directions. An artist has four heartbeats, four callings: *Remember the world. Witness the world. Testify the world. Imagine (create) the world.* Life is an artist with no fear. This is why it keeps birthing beauty.

Let dance be your testimony. It is your soul that dances. Your body just goes along for the ride. Feel the Creation song. Listening is a healing art. Movement is a form of prayer, a door opening, the draft created, an earnest invitation for change to enter your life. Spin, leap, twirl. Let your passion breathe. And let go. Release is an art that pays in peace.

With life, you are given paint and canvas, and the freedom to create works that hang in the gallery of your soul. With your tenderness, you are painting a single, immeasurable mural of Love. Drop all other concerns. Make Love and healing your art. Your legacy. Your life.

Soul growth is a fine art with no name. You know its presence by the divine music it sings. Curate your own soul. Grow a gallery that wonderfully displays and preserves your prized truth. Resuscitate your soul. Love projects are the best kind of art. You are a masterpiece.

Harmony in nature is a continuous state of celebration. Celebration is the breath of joy released by anything when in harmony. And what in your life should you celebrate? Everything. If you are not celebrating, you are suffocating. Celebrate, and you resuscitate.

Celebrate relentlessly. If a single hair on your head behaves, tell it, *I am so proud of you*. Then invite it to go wild, to go dancing. Celebrate a positive thought, a new habit. Celebrate your breath, your skin, your daily endurance. Celebrate the many Love rivers coursing through your life. The way sunlight treats your heart. The taste of food. That you can taste life at all.

Write letters to the spirit in you. Start one with, *Dear Dance, please come alive in me today*. Another with, *Dear Curiosity, how about we discover something new*? Write your letters freely, by the thousands, with words or simply the ink of your heart.

Keep your creative, Love spirit open and flowing. What a thing it is to birth and be born. Life is a sculpture. You are its sculptor. Make something beautiful. Don't chase creativity. Grow calm, still, quiet, and open. Creativity will bloom. Don't force. Feed. Art is a Lover. You know your part. Touch everything gently. Let your thoughts run out to the meadow and play. Wind paints water as thoughts paint your soul.

Your Brilliance

Because your intelligence is often unwanted, want it. Neglected intelligence can turn to madness, to unmoored wandering and house-of-mirrors illusion. Want your intelligence. Stretch it into new languages, new ways of seeing. Make music with it. Go out to what you believe is its boundary, then jump over the fence and run. You will see: No fence exists. You cannot get hurt.

Don't be shy with your brilliance. Anyone who is more attracted to a less intelligent version of you is not for you. Do not hide your intelligence. Some want girls and women to be ashamed of their intelligence. Such shame causes people to vacate their brilliance and live limited lives, stuffed like overgrown crabs into shells too small for their *skyfullness*. Skyfullness is a quality of endless giftedness. A boundless quality. A greatness. If you are a sky and you live like a meager pocket of air, you and all who Love you miss your possible life.

Discover your capability. When your brilliance graduates, enroll in a new program. Intelligence is meant to protect you and to feed your world. When you play down your intelligence to fit in, you are fitting yourself out of your wellness, creating obstructions in your life river, backing up your vital waters. Want your intelligence. Take it places. It will take you to a life of dreams.

Humor

Your laughter is a blessing fountain. You possess two laughters. One is a laughter of seeing. The other a laughter of saying, of singing. Both need your nurturing. See things humorously. Give yourself permission. Share how you see. Tell the stories. Pour out your humor freely. Kill the seeds in you that say what a woman is supposed to be. Reject being tame. Tameness is offspring of ownership. Redefine words like *proper, classy, graceful* to include the big, billowing circus of your humor.

When you use humor out of nervousness, it can calm your nerves. It can also cause you to be hurtful, and to create dis-ease in others. Pay attention to what is surging out of you. Laughter does not justify harm. Loving care justifies laughter.

You know how you feel when people do not feed their children, or even water their plants. Don't let them say you never feed your laughter. Let them say, *I Love the way you always send your laughter to bed belly full.*

Fitness

Consider your fitness. Fit to do what, to be what, to endure what? Let no one tell you what fitness is. Find gifted listeners who can help you hear your own voice. You have a fitness in you that only you may know. It is a fine tuning you recognize in its presence and absence.

Are you fit for the relationships you choose? Are you fit to release the ones whose time has come? Are you fit to stand before a mirror and not judge your fitness? Are you fit to enjoy your exercise and activity? Are you fit for the moment? The moment has much to share with you.

Are you open, pliant, fluid, strong? Your body's fitness is foundation for and results from your soul fitness. Your heart muscle is a foundation of your fitness. Love is the most ancient, powerful, authentic yoga pose. Your mind and heart are partners in this dance. Are you fit to speak gently? Listen kindly? React in healing ways? Who have your fitness instructors been? Scan your life. Gather your roster. Assess its fitness to instruct your fitness. A canyon of difference exists between being fit and pitching a fit.

Your muscles are an awesome gift. You have no need to fear them. Movement and function allow you to experience this world with deep sensitivity. To be in touch and to be touched. Keeping your muscles strong and fluid keeps your life strong and fluid. Your body wants muscle. Literally. Muscle keeps it alive, is a vital piece of the system flow. Embrace your power. All of it.

Addiction steals your life. Even addiction to Love robs you of Love. Desperation cannot live with peace. They cannot be neighbors. Find your courage, daughter, and testify to those you trust of your addictions. Their kinship strengthens you for your separation act. Cleave yourself. No matter how long it takes or how many times you feel you have failed, sharpen your compassion-knife and free yourself from your adhesions. Fly away from your favorite nests. Return when your eyes are new and your heart beats without panicked obsession. Keep breaking your chains. Burn your entanglements.

The food you eat creates your life. In this world, everything is eating everything. What is the spirit of your eating? What are you eating? What are you allowing to eat you? Are you consuming life? How else can you have life in you? How you exist determines whether you yourself are health food or junk food for the world. Diet works both ways. Don't just eat. Truly feed yourself.

With each bite, make an offering of your life. Not just for the life that offered itself for you. Offer yourself to those who suffer, who go without food or clean water or shelter, or Love or kindness. Your nutrition isn't just to satisfy your appetite. It exists to fuel you to serve. To use your life energy and brain and body to feed the world.

Gratitude

Filled with gratitude, your soul has no room for anything that is not Love. Gratitude is how sacred Love acts inside a soul. It is possible to be so grateful that the heart dissolves into all of life and remains there, smiling. If the fruit that is your heart ripens and swells with Love's ultimate sugar, no other element can get inside. Oh, to be an orchard resistant to pestilence. A human being awash in an ecstasy of praise and worship. Let glory rummage through your soul and show you what it finds.

Where you go, bring your own blessings. See the gifts you have and are. Seeing creates more gifts. Learn to see the blessing in all things, and you will know the blissing in all ways. Be a mobile oasis. Drop sacred seeds.

If you see someone who has good light,
thank them for it. It will help them
keep the light on.

Make it your passion project to look for gifts around you. As you live, your spirit will rise and fall like ocean waves. Give thanks for this movement. Let it grow gentle. You are a music sent from beyond. These are your notes. This is your song.

Warm summer nights beneath a half-blushed moon are wealth enough. Your moments are not impoverished. You can be, by not giving yourself to those moments. Make of yourself an offering to life. Finally feel alive. Praise your life. Good things will grow from the watering.

Peace comes to rest in gratitude the way a petal comes to rest on water. Let gratitude's gentle river carry your peaceful heart to where sunlight dances and natural creatures play.

All that you are is inseparable from all that is. Weep gratitude. Gratitude deepens the soul. Soul work deepens gratitude. Round and round it goes. When you change your prayer to gratitude, your prayer changes you to peace.

From this day forward, the young girl would wake and wash her soul with these words: *I am blessed. I am a living blessing. I choose to deliver the gift.*

Your Courage

Fear can be a dictator. A killer of souls. A genocidal force. Fear can also be a friend. What you do with your personal fear counts. Do not fear your fear. Fear not knowing your fear. Not being honest with yourself about how it lives in you. You have reasons for doing things and not doing things. Whatever those reasons are, fear is often at the root. Minding your fear is helpful daily practice. Do you fear losing things? Jobs, Lovers, reputation, acceptance, belonging? Many of us lose these very things *because* we fear losing them. A fear paradox and self fulfilling prophecy.

Fear is foreign to flowers.
Which is why they blossom.

Fear is rarely a good life strategy, business plan, or relationship model. Fear can burn down your whole life. Or it can lift you into the stratosphere of true change. It depends on you. Some cannot stand this responsibility. Others Love the opportunity. Notice the difference in words. *Responsibility* may feel heavy. *Opportunity*, light. If this is true for you, see fear as an opportunity and you will rise like helium.

Know your sacred, innate power. Fear is not a problem of powerlessness. It is a byproduct of perception. Whether under a full moon or at sunrise, keep wading into your ocean of truth. Acclimate. Get to know your big water nature. Perceive your capacity to wash away sand castles and leave all things glistening from your touch.

A mountain of courage will rise from your fear, if only you would exercise your faith. Your fear is a sand castle. Your truth is an ocean. Live in your truth. What fear builds is brittle, inflamed, and impotent. What faith builds is alive with everlasting light, fertile as the sun.

Overthrow your fears.
The only revolution that matters.

Beware those who live so long in fear that they violently oppose freedom. Theirs. And yours. Graciously end your relationship with fear. It keeps raising its price, promising benefits that become burdens. It pollutes your mind day and night. Take off your robes of fear. It is time for nakedness and pure dancing only your heart can do.

Your Power

I admire you as you live in your power, freeing your innate energy and light, your singular intuition and way of seeing. I am humbled by the way you go about being you, and not being what you are not. Animals and plants are great at not being what they are not. We often falter.

When you courageously visit your pain, *that* is your power. The healing that comes is your power. Your silence when others are lost in fits of noise is your power. Your power gushes out when you cry purely. When you laugh until you cry. When injustice crosses your sky and you shoot it down with an arrow of integrity. When you bleed, dance, care, remember, you are in your power.

When you resist your power, I see you suffer. Anyone who cares can see you suffer. Fighting your power in order to fit in and belong, you suffer. Avoiding your fear of your power and what it brings causes you to suffer. Daughter, look deeply into your resistance and see the roots of your suffering. This world suffers from your resistance. Pushing against yourself, you destroy yourself.

When you sandpaper your own soul, you bleed. If you have a deep habit of resisting yourself, you can end the habit. You can give it permission to leave you. Say, *You can go now.* These words are simple. Their power enormous. If you mean the words. Notice the ease of your life when you are in your power, wearing your power, walking and speaking and acting your power. Notice the effort and pain in your river of resistance. Grow familiar with the sight of your power.

You are a soft thing. Made of spirit and space and light and Love. You are a solid thing. Mountain, muscle, sculpture. All of this is your power. Set it free. *Passive* and *assertive* are only words. You know when you are blooming and when you are shrinking. You know what those feel like. Train yourself to bloom.

When you are in your power, you are a fire starter in a cold land. You walk out at night under the hidden moon and leave it brightly blushing as if kissed by a thousand suns. This does not even touch the boundary of your gift. When you unpeel the moon, the light that falls out is a joy that also lives in the sky of your heart. You too are an illuminated thing. Imagine the tides you bring to dance.

Nothing you ever experience will be in spite of being a woman. You are not disabled. You are supernaturally abled. What are your powers? Keep asking, keep answering. Never stop. Say your power, to hear your own voice. Activate your power, to witness. Be your power, to no longer have to say it.

You are an ancient tree of infinite root and fruit. Many will seek to bring you down, frightened by your grandeur. Stay upright. You are able. Regret hurts when you realize you were able all along but failed to see it, to believe in it. See your able nature. Stare into it more than you stare at your body and face, more than you stare at your Lover. Develop a gaze for your immeasurable able-ness.

They told her to shrink.
So she bloomed into a million suns.

You are spirit. Within this are many elements. Come into your woman spirit. Your power lives only in your spirit. Step out of that, and your power falters. Crystals gather sunlight and make song. You hold those crystals and your own power wakes. This can work the other way around. Gather your power and make medicine. Whatever holds you will take in your medicine, make its own new life.

Permission

Find your true nature, unmeasured by the nature of others. Give yourself permission to *be*—unaltered, undiluted, and unmodified. Do this, and at last you are free, and a dearly needed example of freedom. Many witness your choice of liberation. Freedom is one of the most awesome contagions of all.

They will tell you that you shouldn't reach for the stars. Tell them you are a star. You are reaching for yourself. You cannot be whole until you feel worthy and able of being whole. You deserve peace. Say the words.

Weary of submitting,
she gave her soul permission.
She never stopped soaring.

To achieve healing, freedom, peace, and dreams, you need only give yourself permission. This births a tidal flood of growth and providence that makes all things new. The power of permission is that it recruits your soul drive.

No drive is greater than this. On your lips are words to make your dreams come true. Speak them. Say, *I can.*

Your Voice

Your voice is not weak. Neither are you. Seeds have been planted in you that do not belong. Shame, guilt, stigma, subservience, fear. The more you practice being mute, the more you please the desires of others who wish to impose their voice over your own. When you speak, you ignite girls and women who needed just one more ember to start their own freedom fire.

When you speak to yourself, your heart should bloom. Even in winter you can stir the wildflowers in your heart. Take care of your language. When you adopt the words your oppressor calls you, this is not empowerment. Not art. Not resistance. Not brilliance or genius or pride. It is imitation. Capitulation. Slavery. When you swallow poisonous seeds, those seeds spawn in you, in your children, in your generations.

Oppression is a virus seeking a host. Once you become that host, oppression laughs. It knows it doesn't need to hold you down. You will do that yourself. Use your own sacred language. Tend your sacredness. Grow fluent in Love. Be a translator for the masses who have had their language stolen. Your soul speaks endless Love languages. Learn them all. Speak for the world.

Sink your Love into your soil. Find the seeds, cradle them as you pull them up out of you. Go back inside and water the tender, trembling seed that carries your song. You know the one. Bring it out into the world. You need your voice. We need your music. This life is a symphony.

Allow your language to mature with the rest of you. If you are an adult, talking like a child doesn't suit you. It only steals the influence you are meant to have on your people's sacred tongue. Use your beautiful language.

Say your words. People need to hear you say what you feel, what you are thinking, and how they can and cannot treat you. If you wait for them to guess, imagine, intuit, or receive in their dreams your truth, you may wait forever. Dropping hints and hoping can be a passive, disempowering, ineffective approach.

You have the right to be direct. This is how you treat your sacredness. You speak it. If you do not, other voices will be all too happy to speak for you. Then your life becomes their truth, or worse, their dishonoring intention for your life. If you speak out loud, with grace and spirit, you create a life climate in *your* image. People will know how to walk your sacred lands. Loving yourself is to say yourself, out loud or however your soul decides.

I knew a woman once, out in the far desert. She knew something meaningful. That words are clay pots. Baskets. Jars. They hold things. Should not be poured out carelessly. Are better when infused with honeysuckle petals and lemon zest. And with care can come to hold an entire people in their bellies. She learned to care for them. Words. When to use them. How to move them up from her chest, through the bellows of her mouth, over her braille tongue and autumn lips. This brought miracles. Gardens grew around her, wherever she was. Gardens of such beauty that most every soul she encountered was left wonderfully wordless.

When you give your stories birth, they flow unto the world, a fountain that feeds new gardens, lush forests, paradises of meaning. When you hold your stories tight and tense inside, they calcify, and you become a soul of cysts. Your living design is to be a free river, your language and dreams splashing on drier shores, blessing seed into sprout that does not fathom life without the wondrous hallmark of inspiration.

Daughter, your words are pregnant with meaning and medicine. Sometimes, your voice is silence. When you speak in your soul's native tongue, you finally make sense to you. When you open your precious mouth, let only Love come out. Keep speaking Love words.

———

A woman touches her chest, feeling the joy in her heart. Beneath the humming blue sky, she feels sun melt into her skin, as though she is swimming the warm ocean of sky and light. A breeze cools her, touching soft memories her spirit now offers up. She breathes a contented breath and thinks: *This moment right here is the summer of my life. It is good.* She knows the next moment, if she lets it, will be summer, too. A river rises in her, spills out as words:

I am not a language you speak in harsh tones. I am poetry, lush and mystic. Whisper me in moonlight. Sing me in sanctuary. Cry me on the mountain in a chant of breeze. Elope with your passion. Meet me in the meadow of starlight and galaxies. I will marry you to your Greatest Love. But first... whisper me.

This that I am is a gentle place. A kind space. It is sacred. Clean. Pure. Soft and tender and safe. You can rest here. Just don't pollute it. Treat it as a sanctuary. Come and kneel. Say prayers and sing. Drink from the fountain. Lie upon the soft moss. Partake of the endless sky. Warm your bones in the sun. Take pleasure in the fragrance. Feel the calming breeze. Listen to the silence and song. Laugh here. Cry here. Wade in the blessing waters. Remember yourself. Come and go, but never claim or clench. I am a forest of trees. A sonnet of river. This is a gentle place. You are welcome here. Gently.

Your Influence

The ancient one grew fatigued, even as his heart engorged with Love. He took a deeper breath and continued:

Pay attention to who you are choosing as role models. You have many of them. Most you never meet. You see them in stores, on the street, in stories. You make subtle decisions as you watch them, sublime contracts in the soul: *I want to be like that. I want to look like that, act like that, have what she has.* Pay close attention. These people aren't just having an impression on you. They are leading you places. Do you want to go there? What do you sense those places have done to them?

Learn to look closely into the souls of those you admire or envy. Do you feel suffering there? Peace? What do you truly want, suffering or peace? Role modeling is an agreement. We decide together that we'll all go this way or that way, but what does the way, and the destination, do to us? And what if you choose to go another way? What are you role modeling then? People are watching you far more often than you realize. You are likely to underestimate your influence. People of all ages are finding their next fashion in you.

In every single moment of your life, you are a wonder of the world to other girls and women beholding you. No matter the depths of your self criticism and insecurity, you are a mountain of light being watched by other women fixated on your peaks and valleys.

Boys and men are watching, too. They are consumed with knowing what you will allow, and how they are to treat you. They also watch you to decipher how they are to treat themselves, what they are to allow. A secret that women and men rarely speak out loud is that we are models for each other. Across the mystic plains of not being one thing, we are entranced by the mystery of those we are not.

Those others hold a power over us, an opportunity to impress upon us their way of being. And if their way of being is self destructive and self demeaning, seeds are born in us. Seeds of our own self regard, and ones that light our imagination of those other mysterious ones.

Once I heard a woman laughing. She sounded like a crow crowing. Seconds after, I saw a crow fly over. It was crowing. All living things are in tune with each other, so attracted, that you can create the climate of your life. Your influence is greater than you ever know.

Don't wait to teach peace until you have mastered it. Peace is a wild horse. You will never ride it perfectly. But if you have been touched by its power, teach peace.

Some call your influence *leadership*. What are you leading yourself to? Have you done your homework on your intended destination? How do things work there, what is the climate, how about the local economy? In other words, don't show up an ignorant tourist suddenly wailing in culture shock and offending the locals because this place isn't what you imagined. Instead, be informed of where in life you are leading yourself. Come prepared.

True Wealth

If the dog you walk grows powerful enough, the dog will walk you. Money is an idea. It can infect the mind and overrun the soul with desperation. It can also be an instrument you keep polished and cared for, to fulfill its purpose as you need. If you let your money pull you along in a river of obsession, such a river leads to strange, fallow lands where nothing real grows.

Money is not the root of independence. Independence is the root of independence. When you know how to exist, unafraid and free, you are ready to be in a relationship with money that serves your soul. Money does not make your family secure. Security is a wealth born of healthful choices and ways of seeing and being. Money does not grant you power. True power keeps money-mindedness from becoming an invasive species. This kind of power is staying power. Stay in your truth, your soul, your center, regardless of the money-weather that comes and goes.

Financial independence is not about being able to boast, *I don't need a man, or a woman.* It has little to do with others, and everything to do with your wellness. How are you flowing? How fruitful is your engagement with life and the world? How are you offering your gifts, and what is their imprint? *Independence* is not even the most healthful word. You have no need to create a money bubble for yourself. You do not benefit from becoming an isolated, self serving individual, cut-off from others.

Financial fruitfulness, or just *fruitfulness*, may be a better term. Are you applying your full greatness to your life and the world? Are your relationships supporting you in the callings you are drawn to? How is earning income in the way you are affecting your spirit, your health? Are you staying in touch with your many work possibilities? Yes, appraise your spending habits. But make sure to include how you spend your energy, Love, intelligence, humor, kindness, curiosity, and courage. How are you spending your creativity, voice, and inspiration? Are you creating fertile grounds that enrich your relationships, stabilize your income, and balance your attachment to material things?

Financial independence suggests a kind of hoarding. You may become great at hoarding, but the money pile you obsess over can consume you. It is easy to become a prisoner to money and fear of losing it. Tend to your financial fruitfulness. Are your people, your community, and your humanity fruitful? How are you adding to the tribal fruitfulness that ultimately decides your own?

You can invest in financial games and risks. But what is the relationship between your actual labor and servitude, and the rivers that run back through your life and lands? Farmers understand this. What you invest in soil, seed, water, and light, births your bounty. Farm your life. You can make many things grow, and grow for good cause, if you apply your native intelligence and care.

Care enough. Not only that you are financially secure, but that you are living in a circle of growing human security. Some seasons in your life, you will support the circle in its dire need. Other seasons, you will pray the circle is wealthy enough in every way to support you. Money in the end is not a competitive reality, no matter what people believe. It is a question put to humanity: *How will you care for each other? How will you endure and thrive?*

Travel

When you have an impulse to go somewhere, to discover the world, first try visiting your soul. The travel is cheap, and the destination couldn't be more suited for you. You can find as much meaning sitting in silence all day next to a flower as you can traveling the world. What matters is that you give yourself to what you accompany.

If you listen to some people, you might never go anywhere, afraid for what might happen to you *as a woman*. Fear need not be your dictator. Fear cannot reject your passport or detain you. Only people can do that. Tell yourself stories of your safety, and your mind and spirit will be meadows lush with feelings of safety.

If you have travel fever, cure your fever. You are capable of traveling safely. If you believe travel is your savior, your salvation from your troubles, you may find that travel introduces you to your troubles over and over again, an undesired matchmaker that stalks you.

If you believe your spirit can heal you as you travel, you are likely to be affirmed. No place in the world possesses your perfect medicine if you are not willing to be cured. You can try to run from yourself sitting in a classroom, in traffic, or in a distant land. Traveling or not makes no difference. All running is a delusion, a cruel seduction.

If you can sit still at home in peace, you can travel within that stillness and experience wonders beyond this world. And if you can travel to other countries and cultures with humility and openness, you can find a stillness you have never known.

Traveling globally or inwardly, do it joyfully, as your soul conductor inspires. Travel alone. Travel in hordes. Travel with your heart hanging out of your chest. Lose your language. Start speaking strange tongues. Eat new foods. Lose old tastes. Move in with the locals and let them teach you their life. For at least part of your travel, have no schedule. Let the moments come.

Abundance

Your life is an abundant life. This is true regardless of circumstance. You are walking through a fruitful orchard, sometimes seeing with the wrong eyes, causing you not to recognize the fruit. The more you reach for, pluck, and taste the fruit of your life, the better you will be at reaching, plucking, tasting. Yet if you do not see the fruit as fruit, no harvesting skill will help you.

Stillness gives you true vision for fruit-seeing. Slow down. Step away from the carnival. Take a deep breath outside the circus tent. Stay in your spirit and you will see this world for what it is, and sacredness for what it offers. Be like a child who goes wandering in the forest and ends up with the juice of wild berries all over her smiling face.

It occurred to the young woman that poverty of the soul is a choice away from becoming a soulful abundance. She realized her state of deprivation was a habitual drought, a long season of not piercing her own heart with her own Love, or with life's bounty. She let the rains come. A whole new paradise bloomed inside.

Living Miraculously

Every single thing about you is a living miracle. A phenomenon delicate and precise. A happening that could easily not have happened. You have every right and reason to spend your life in awe and wonder. Awe and wonder are kindling for the joy fire your heart was designed to host. Pick up a grain of sand. Gaze into the universe it holds. Look out into the universe at night. See the starlight your soul has inspired.

Simplicity is a Love offering from you to you. A gift of lightness. Wrapped in quiet splendor and unadorned ease. Infinite miracles are happening all at once. Let them all make you laugh and cry. Especially the one that is you. Your soul, too, is a wonder of the world. Proceed. Move. Dare. Decide. Let go. Often, movement is the first step in a miracle.

As an ancient one, I have seen every particle of the universe. You do not yet know the miracle you are. Your life quivers in a brilliant web of everything. Have hope. See beyond your fear valley. Beyond the horizon live endless peaks of joy. Wade out into the peace water of your life. When the water reaches your waist, dive down all the way. Your soul is an ocean. Swim the deep.

Sunlight kissed her shoulder.
A reminder that joy lives in the simplest things.

You are the dawn of spring. Fragrance after rain. Joy in the valley. Breeze on the mountain. Sun upon souls. What makes flowers open and meadows hum. You give life to this earth. You, phenomenal, extraordinary atmosphere. The most Loving thing you can do for yourself is to show up. For your moments. Your feelings. Your truth. Your life. Spend your life deciphering the riddle, the code you are. Do it laughing. Do it joyfully.

If you count all the true miracles of your life, you may never stop weeping gratitude. Your life is not a series of days. It is a river of miracles. Nothing is more enormous than the smallest things. Find yourself in everything. Dissolve the boundaries of your heart. Today, decide to see beauty everywhere. Be a finder of miracles. Blush more. Sip your moments like tea. Savor the miracle that is your life.

A young prophet spoke to her grandmothers, saying, *We are in that time of day. When sun, like a lonely flame, draws nearer and shadows bloom from their burrows to lay out their carpet for night. We are in a great turning, a mystic enterprise, a serenade between soulful things.* Her grandmothers listened. They knew the path they had tread was coming to a place of healing. New moons and suns would rise. Blessing water would run. They exhaled.

The ancient one concluded:

Daughters, I have been praying for you since before your spirit entered this world. I will not stop. I will keep pouring Love. I Love you with such an awesome ache. But you must Love yourself. I pray you take off your old mental clothing. Lay down your ancestral burdens. Let your ancient pain evaporate and go on its way. You have long been awash in what was not yours. Now it is time for you to carry your soul into the light.

The valley cooled as shadows spread. The women sang a silent song. Arms around their daughters, they bobbed side-to-side, a soft tide. The ancient one grew quiet. He bowed to his many daughters. Water poured from his quietude. No energy was left in him. Spirit was done with his vessel for this moment of sun rise and set.

This day, the ancient one shared a truth already living in his daughters. He had returned to them their own exclamation, stilling their water. They saw their reflection and remembered. Now his body turned to light and merged with them, for they had birthed the light he was. Women and their daughters and granddaughters and great granddaughters laughed and cried together. They drummed earth with their bare feet and soulfully sang an unprecedented song. Blue sky fattened with white clouds. Trees leaned toward the revival. Rains came with their hopeful conversation. The women opened their mouths to the sky. And they did drink the water.

If this book touched you, you can touch it back.

Please consider writing an **online reader review** at Amazon, Barnes & Noble, or Goodreads. Reviews are a valuable way to support the life of a book and especially to support an independent author.

Freely **post social media photos** of you or others with the book, just the book itself, or passages from the book. Please kindly include the hashtag **#JAIYAJOHN.**

I cherish your support of my books and our Soul Water Rising rehumanizing mission around the world.

BOOK ANGEL PROJECT

Your book purchases support our global *Book Angel Project,* which provides scholarships and book donations for vulnerable youth, and places gift copies of my inspirational books throughout communities worldwide, to be discovered by the souls who need them. The books are left in places where hearts are tender: hospitals, nursing homes, prisons, wellness centers, group homes, mental health clinics, and other community spaces.

If you are fortunate to discover one of our *Book Angel* gift books, please kindly post a photo of you with the book on Instagram, using the hashtag **#JAIYAJOHN**, or email it to us at **books@soulwater.org.** Thank you!

I Will Read for You:
The Voice and Writings of Jaiya John

A podcast. Voice medicine to soothe your soul, from poet, author, and spoken word artist Jaiya John. Bedtime bliss. Morning meditation. Daytime peace. Comfort. Calm. Soul food. Come, gather around the fire. Let me read for you. **Spotify. Apple. Wherever podcasts roam.**

Dr. **Jaiya John** shares freedom work and healing messages with audiences worldwide. He was orphan-born in the desert of New Mexico, is a former professor of social psychology at Howard University, and has lived in various locations, including Kathmandu, Nepal. Jaiya is the author of numerous books, and the founder of Soul Water Rising, a global rehumanizing mission supporting the healing and wholeness of vulnerable and oppressed populations.

Jacqueline V. Carter and Kent W. Mortensen served graciously, faithfully, and skillfully as editors for *Freedom*. I am forever grateful for their Love labor.

Secure a Jaiya John keynote or talk:

jaiyajohn.com/speaking

OTHER BOOKS BY JAIYA JOHN

Jaiya John titles are available online where books are sold. To learn more about this and other books by Jaiya, to order **discounted bulk quantities**, and to learn about Soul Water Rising's global freedom work, please visit us at:

jaiyajohn.com

books@soulwater.org

@jaiyajohn (IG FB TW YT)